AUTHENTIC SENSUAL LIVING

Authentic

Sensual

LIVING

Your Guide to Igniting all Your Senses
and Enriching Your Life

CHARLYN BELLUZZO

Afterword by Georges M. Halpern, MD PhD., *The Case for Pleasure*

Authentic Sensual Living
Your Guide to Igniting All Your Senses and Enriching Your Life

Published by
Amorosa Bella
88 King Street, #1205, San Francisco, CA 94107

Paperback:
ISBN 13: 978-0-578-01253-7

Hardcover:
ISBN 13: 978-0-578-03204-7

Book Design: Karrie Ross www.KarrieRoss.com Los Angeles, CA
Editing: Deborah Roth www.deborahroth.com
Photography:
Cover photo: Henry Hargreaves www.henryhargreaves.com New York, NY
Author photo: Sylvia Steininger www.sylviasphotography.com SF, CA
Logo Illustration: Jason Parker Design www.jsnprkr.com Oakland, CA

"Sensuality"
describes the essence
of experiencing
the full spectrum of emotions
using all six
of your senses:

sight

sound

smell

taste

touch

and intuition.

TABLE of CONTENTS

Message from the Author

This is your guide to experiencing life fully through all of your senses. Mastering your ability to "feel" results in enjoying a rich and sensual life.

Welcome back to your senses!

As you take this journey with me through my book, you will master your ability to "feel." The two most important principles are that:

- The quality of your life is measured in **moments** of living, not years of life.
- You can experience each moment of your life through **all your senses**, often on multiple levels at the very same time.

My book takes a "storytelling" approach to learning, sharing many examples from my experiences and the experiences of others; allowing you to reflect on our own view of the world and then provides a platform to design your own authentic sensual living plan.

The internationally recognized author, physician, and health researcher, Dr. Georges Halpern (incidentally the author of the afterword section to this book) relates a story that was told to him by the Michael Oliver, a splendid chef and impressive author of cookbooks for adults and children.-

The story goes like this:

> "On a long stretch of beach with crashing surf, a young lad runs barefoot in sand, tethered to his soaring kite's string. The boy notices in the distance a silhouette of a man standing at the edge of the water. As the boy flies his kite down the beach closer to the figure he stops dead in his tracks. The kite falls limp on the sand as the boy stands awestruck beside his discovery. Hand-drawn in the wet sand are numerous works of art: astonishingly beautiful portraits, castles, flowers, women dancing, a dream-like gallery of original art. This spellbinding sight immobilizes the boy and tears of joy fill his eyes. He marvels at each of the drawings, each one as striking as the next, as he slowly closes the distance between himself and the genius artist, the old man at the edge of the water. The young lad wants to express his sense of being enchanted but before he is able to do so a sudden and huge wave pummels the beach where the drawings lay and the scenes are instantly erased. The boy smiles and picks up his kite as the old man smiles back as they both leave the beach. The man: Pablo Picasso."

The quality of your life is measured moment to moment. Experience its richness now, for in the next moment, it may all be gone. Waves of change crash in on us continually during the course of our lives. Some waves we welcome as positive change and some are less pleasant, bringing hardship or sorrow. The richness of life is a swinging pendulum; both bitter and sweet situations add spice and balance to our human existence.

The story above takes place on a beach in Southern France. Try reading it again invoking all of your senses: smell the salty tang of the sea, hear the gulls cry and the whistle of the wind, feel the moist air around your face and the coarse sand under your feet, see the waves curl and the clouds float by overhead. And don't forget the moment of seeing the beautiful transitory pictures drawn in the sand by Pablo Picasso.

One Important fact to remember throughout this book is how you think of the words "sensual, sensually, and sensuality." You'll read more about these words in Chapter Four (Living Sensually) but in the meantime simply know that I'm using this word in its truest sense, sensual: according to your senses. This includes the five you grew up knowing by heart (taste, touch, sight, sound, and smell) and some of the more esoteric ones: a sixth sense (intuition) and sexual (a lovely enriched combination of senses).

ENJOY!

Moments to Capture from the Prologue

As you master your ability to "feel," the two most important principles are:

- The quality of your life is measured in **moments** of living, not years of life.

- You can experience each moment of your life through **all your senses**, often on multiple levels at the very same time.

CHAPTER ONE

Introduction

Lost in the San Francisco Fog

This is a book of stories that starts with one of my own.

On the day I'm describing I looked impeccable! I was wearing a sleek black St. John knit dress, the same one that Angelina Jolie had worn in last spring's fashion spread, and it hugged my frame perfectly. My Hermès scarf was casually thrown over my shoulders, a gorgeous accent and entirely professional.

My equally gorgeous PowerPoint presentation was neatly stored on my flash memory stick, tucked in the side compartment of my black leather briefcase. I was ready.

Ready for what? That's the question. As the stylish wife of a technology executive, I had been invited to join an early stage venture capital firm as a senior partner. Not because I'm trained in finance and have a proven investment track record, the usual qualifications needed. Quite the contrary! My biography on the firm's website emphasizes my years of experience in global health research and my work with international Non Government Organizations (NGOs). It was clear to me, no illusion: it was my husband's ability to make a significant investment in the fund that guaranteed my role in the firm.

Nonetheless, that morning, I confidently strutted out of my building on the corner of King Street and the Embarcadero, rehearsing my pitch to a cluster of potential investors over and over in my mind. I walked briskly toward my Range Rover, parked across the street at Pier 38 next to the South Beach Yacht Club.

Mark Twain famously said that the coldest winter he ever experienced was summer in San Francisco. It's a witty, pithy comment and one that visitors to San Francisco hear endlessly. But this was not one of those foggy chilly summer days. This was a clear day, an unusually warm, brilliantly sunny, summer day along the waterfront in San Francisco. There was not a breath of wind. Sunlight shimmered through the palm trees that line the center median of Embarcadero Street. The often rough and murky water of San Francisco Bay glistened curiously like glass.

I didn't notice the exquisite beauty around me as I glided down the sidewalk toward the crosswalk.

The San Francisco Muni Train emerged from the underground several blocks before my crossing. The light for pedestrians glared solid red and the no-crossing signal flashed "caution!" on and off, on and off. The bright white "Train Approaching" signal beamed.

I stepped off the curb to cross; fully preoccupied with rehearsing my script.

The ground beneath my feet trembled like the beginning of a California earthquake as the Muni Train barreled down the track.

I kept walking, oblivious - though there was no way I could not have seen the Muni Train approaching my intersection; horn blaring; conductor leaning halfway out the window, waving frantically shouting, "Get off the track!" The train had already passed the final point of stopping before the intersection.

I don't remember slowly stepping back or the train storming by within inches of my face.

I do remember standing still, then, trembling,

I was so disconnected I couldn't even cry.

I aimlessly wandered my way back up King Street to my building, dismissing my business presentation without even an apologetic phone call.

Once back inside my home, I began to consider what had just happened.

Where the Story Really Began

Step back with me about a decade in my story. This part of my tale begins at the "happy ending" point of most stories.

I was a young and ambitious single woman, a mother of two young children from a previous marriage, making my professional way in a "man's world" of medicine and pharmaceutical research.

It was the beginning of a typical business week for me. I was flying to the East coast on a Sunday evening, United Airlines flight 338, planning to prepare for a series of grueling research meetings during the flight.

I was heading to Georgetown University School of Medicine, Department of Physiology and Biophysics and Professor Harry G. Preuss, MD. You NEVER wanted to appear before Dr. Preuss anything less than over-prepared. A long cross-country flight was exactly the seclusion I needed to get ready for the week ahead.

As I sat in my reclusive mindset, a friendly interruption from my seatmate in 2B, sometimes known as the Shakespeare seat (2B or not 2B...) felt particularly annoying. Trapped against the window in seat 2A, I had no choice but to look up from my notebook and return small talk.

As a female "road warrior," the title we frequent fliers bestow on ourselves, those of us who spend a great portion of our professional lives traveling to the destinations where work takes place, I had learned to erect a brick wall between myself and those who found picking up women on airplanes some type of sport.

Yet it was impossible to ignore the fact that there was something special about this particular businessman. He was a little different. His incredibly warm smile, relaxed and confident nature, unique depth of business acumen, clever wit, and boyish charm soon had me fixated on our "small talk" conversation.

Just before landing, this intriguing businessman handed me his card. I did not reciprocate; it was my habit to never give my contact information away on an airplane or in a bar.

This interesting man had been an executive at Hewlett Packard (HP) for many years and was currently CEO of a company called Silicon Graphics (SGI); I naively had never heard of this company. He suggested that if I were ever in the San Francisco Bay Area with my children that we were welcome to visit his research and development lab, filled with lots of virtual technology. "Kids love the virtual lab," he said with assurance.

I thanked him for his card and slipped it into my briefcase. We exited the plane and I watched this impressive stranger walk down the concourse out of sight, never turning around to notice I was watching him.

At the end of the week, I hopped on another plane and returned home to my children. My son, Riley, asked how my week went. I remembered the business card that my seatmate had given me. I said that I had met this computer guy on the flight out to DC last Sunday and that he was an executive of some high tech company who said he had a cool research lab with a lot of virtual technology stuff and we were invited to visit the lab sometime.

Riley took the card in both hands and shook it at me like he had just won the lottery. "Mother," he exclaimed, "How did you do this?!"

I said, "Do you know this guy?"

He sarcastically replied, "Um, do you *know* of *Star Wars* or *Jurassic Park?* His company did all the cool animation for those films! These guys are computer Gods!"

It looked like my seatmate was right.

As you would expect, that night I wrote an email to my intriguing seatmate and we scheduled a visit to SGI's research lab.

Bright New Beginnings

Three years later, we were wed.

Prior to our wedding, he had become the President/COO of Microsoft and moved to Seattle. We started our life together much like a Danielle Steele romance novel crossed with the Brady Bunch, passionately in love with each other in and out of international backdrops and private jets, while struggling to blend our two sets of children.

My new husband, Rick, encouraged me to pursue my dreams so I went back to school to gain an MBA degree at the University of Colorado, Denver. I wanted to understand the business of medicine.

Several years later, Rick became Chairman/CEO of Quantum Corporation. We moved back to the San Francisco Bay Area. I returned to school again, this time to earn a doctorate degree in Public Health and Tropical Medicine at Tulane School of Medicine in New Orleans. I now wanted to "improve the lives of the underprivileged in developing areas of the world" through global health and economic development.

Through Rick's professional position and my reckless ambition I began building a reputation in global health. I found myself seated at the table with powerful women like Melinda Gates, Pam Omidyar, Julia Ormond, and others who spend their time saving lives and improving human conditions all over the planet with their philanthropic and public policy achievements.

I took the podium on frequent occasions, invited to speak as an international health expert at forums around the world. A full-page picture and feature article was published in *Paris Vogue* praising my accomplishments as an activist and global health leader.

The Fog Rolls In

All these accomplishments under my belt and I still felt that I was not "measuring up." My feelings of inadequacy grew to become overwhelming. Is there such a thing as addiction to achievement or was over-productivity just an expression of my insecurity?

My life lacked true authenticity. Moments, days, weeks, and months were passing me by without my noticing. My desire to make a difference in the world was sincere, but I overshot the mark by presenting myself as bigger than I really was. My heart was in the right place, but my resources did not match my philanthropic commitments. I got caught up and confused by playing the role of an international humanitarian, along with the women I deeply admired. What I could legitimately give felt like it was never enough. I continually overpromised.

Organizations, including the United Nations High Commissioner for Refugees (UNHCR) in Geneva, Switzerland invited me to join international advisory boards, as one of the global social elite, with the expectation that large contributions would accompany my advisory role. I couldn't seem to say no to any worthy cause. My self-esteem was taking a nosedive attempting to keep up with my humanitarian peers.

My lack of constraint was flooding over into all aspects of my life. My mantra, drilled into me at an early age by a Grandmother who once told me to aim for being useful, not just ornamental, was, "If there is anything worth doing, it is worth overdoing!" I was over involved in the details of my children's lives, even though all four of them were beyond age twenty-one!

I was overcommitted in my community, a social diva, never turning down an invitation, missing a party, or declining the opportunity to take a trip. As a networking goddess, friends and acquaintances looked to me to facilitate connections. Heroic acts of self-sacrifice became routine.

My extreme behavior annoyed and alarmed my husband. His frustration and concern was justified. Often, in my efforts to please others, he was the one I ignored. Guilt over disappointing and hurting my husband added to my feelings of failure.

The tenuous truth of my personal state of affairs was coming to a dramatic head. I had decided to accept a role as senior partner in the early venture capital firm previously mentioned, at the early onset of the present ugly economic downturn. I was failing to bring value to the firm in my new role. I lacked knowledge and experience in raising venture capital and structuring deals. General marketplace conditions in a downturn challenge even the most seasoned investment firms. I was drowning.

My insecurities were on the rise. To me, the minimum standard was excelling. Over achieving was a family value I was taught while growing up. To top it off, I was heading straight into menopause, complete with all the well known symptoms.

A perfect storm hit me - appropriately in New York City, epicenter of the economic downturn. Seeking professional insight from a seasoned veteran in the field in the quest of secrets to becoming a successful venture capital partner, I became unintentionally and inappropriately emotionally involved with him.

All hell broke loose when my husband read correspondence on my Blackberry between my "insightful advisor" and me!

The pressures of attempting to rebuild my marriage, protect my family, preserve my reputation, build my career, continue my humanitarian interests, and save my own sanity had driven me into a dark and lonely place. I was hopelessly lost in the famous fog of San Francisco...even on the clearest and most sunny days.

And so we are back in full circle, standing by the woman – me – who saw, but did not see, the train bearing down on her. Who felt, but did not feel, beautiful and competent. Who tasted fear, too late. Who heard the rumble of the train only as it was passing in front of her face. And who felt the cold chill of the non-existent fog swirling around her as she walked, unseeingly, back home.

I had denied myself everything, to the point where even my most basic senses had let me down, and to no surprise: what had I done for them lately? If I had been ignoring my husband, how much more dismissive had I been to myself: refusing to participate in the moment, with my focus always on the next ten. My senses were unused to the point of being nothing more than flickering automatic responses, and even they were operating sluggishly. My life was a hard candy shell: shiny and delicious, masking nothing but air within.

How could this have happened? More importantly: how could it be fixed? Most importantly: how many other people were going through the same thing and who could learn to bring their senses alive again, beyond the basics, to the enrichment of their senses and themselves?

This book is written for them. For me. For you.

Moments to Capture from Chapter One

As you master your ability to "feel," maintain open sensory pathways to your emotions by remembering:

- Your senses gather external information from your environment and send it to your brain to trigger your emotions. Your emotions prompt an accurate reaction. If the response pathway between your senses and your emotional reaction is blocked, you are at personal risk.

- The appearance of external perfection does not ensure emotional balance and well-connected internal pathways of response. Your disrupted emotional pathways can be well masked, even from you.

- Internal emotional **imbalance** can happen to anyone, regardless of your position in life, education, social status, or temporal wealth.

CHAPTER TWO

Living "In Touch" in an Increasingly Detached World

Waking Up into the Light of Day

I do not dispute we are living in desperate and uncertain times. I have tremendous concern and compassion for all those living in pain, personal danger, starvation, and extreme poverty, jobless, or homeless, here in the US or abroad.

In 1943 Abraham Maslow, an American behavioral scientist, published an article entitled "A Theory of Human Motivation" in which he argued that people everywhere are subject to what he called a "hierarchy of needs." At the bottom of the pyramid of human needs are food and shelter, sex and sleep: elementary physiological needs. Next are the basic needs for safety and security. As long as these things are lacking – as they are for billions of the world's poor – the search for basic needs dominates every aspect of life.

This book is not written for the benefit of these incredibly disenfranchised people in the greatest need. There are valuable publications and programs sponsored by some of the most brilliant and generous people on the planet today, addressing critical needs of suffering individuals. This book has a different purpose and targets another population: It was written for you.

If you are reading this book, there is a very good chance that you are exactly the type of person that faces challenges of detachment, numbness, and distraction that are addressed in this chapter. Detachment is a contemporary condition of our society that seems to be on the rise.

The author Barbara Holland writes in her book *Endangered Pleasures,* "In subtle and small ways, joy is leaking out of our lives, almost without a struggle."

The current Information Age fires "facts" at us from all directions at lightning speed. Information bombards us through all of our media outlets: film, television, Internet, mobile phone, and even appliances like refrigerators and new washing machines!

Bad news, it seems, always travels faster. In this present time of economic woes and personal uncertainties, we accept bad news as more credible than good news. The media, for the most part, is reactive rather than proactive. Media depends on you and me to complete the feedback loop. What we pay attention and respond to, we receive more of. It is as simple as that!

Survival Detachment

The human psyche was designed to survive. Your mind has been equipped with formidable means of "blocking out" horrific scenes and trauma, enabling you to act upon your reflexes and to preserve your very life. Personal stories from 9-11 survivors bear witness of the overwhelming detachment and disassociation that can occur during times of maximum stress. Below is a personal account from one 9-11 survivor. I am protecting her identity, but her story below is told in her own words:

> "My office was in Tower One... As Information System Audit
> Project Leader and acting head of the department, I arrived at work

as usual around 6:30 a.m., sipped tea as I read and answered my e-mail, reviewed my meeting schedule and prepared other work.

I went to our 29th floor NE conference room around 8:42 a.m. Minutes later, I heard what sounded like the whine of an incoming missile (I thought "are we under attack?" and tried to imagine from where a missile could possibly have been launched!) I heard a thunderous BOOM; the building shook violently and the floor (each floor was approximately one acre in size) did a rolling wave; I saw debris falling past the windows.

The emergency PA system instructed us to evacuate using the staircase. During the descent, we had no idea about what could have happened. A man behind me said he got a message from his wife on his message pager that said a plane had hit the building. We wondered if it was an accident.

I walked across the street and up Fulton. Some people told me they saw the second plane circle around and fly into the second tower. About halfway up the block, I saw a large puddle of something red. It had the consistency of ketchup but was bright red. I saw a pair of cork-soled platform black wedges next to the puddle and a white towel partially soaked in the blood.

A guy I didn't know came up to me and told me I didn't want to know what had been there. I said that I did want to know, please tell me. He said someone's head had landed there and squashed on impact but it had been taken away. He said they couldn't find the body.

A red/white/blue Waterway ferry bus came along and I flagged it. The driver asked me where I was going. I said "NJ". He motioned to come aboard. I talked to the other passengers and listened to their stories. We zigzagged our way across town to the 34th Street pier.

At the pier, there was a crowd of people numbering around 1500. We quickly saw there was only one ferry running. From our location, we could only see the black smoke despite the sky being clear. No one wanted to believe the towers were gone.

At least half of the people on board had been at or near the World Trade Center (WTC) and were wet like me or sooty. We discussed facts about the WTC and our individual experiences that day. One pregnant woman had trekked to the ferry from the WTC on foot carrying a laptop and her purse.

I arrived home around 3:15 p.m., still damp, wrinkled and a little sooty. I sat in the same spot almost constantly for two days watching TV following September 11, 2001.

I had no bad dreams nor do I have any today. I have seen occurrences of the 1960's, having lived in Boston and LA. I experienced earthquakes, wild fires, civil disobedience, and day-to-day violence coupled with what we see at the movies and on TV and I realize I have been left a little numb. Not that I'm not concerned for those who were injured (physically and mentally) and for those who lost their lives...but even being there and seeing it up close there was a disconnect from the reality of it all."

Thank heaven, most of you reading this book were not at Ground Zero on that fateful day, but your psyche is wired with the same emergency response mechanisms and you may have felt a similar "numbness" when facing a situation in your own life that stressed you to your limit.

I shared this story to emphasize that your ability to "detach" can be necessary for your survival and continuing mental and emotional functions. The problem we face in our society today is one of "overusing" your natural detachment mechanism in everyday life.

Universal Detachment

Jonathan Birchall describes this "new texture to everyday life," in his book *Elsewhere USA* as "pervasive social anxiety." I see pervasive social anxiety as the precursor to universal detachment!

I think you know the feeling: you are never fully present in the moment you are living in. Your blackberry is vibrating with a text message, as you fast-forward through television commercials on your previously recorded football game, while your daughter is asking for the car keys, as you worry about the balance on your multiple credit cards and you are unsure what the cramping feeling in your gut is telling you. Are you hungry or is unaddressed anxiety leading to an ulcer? Either case, you have no time to be concerned with the underlying problem causing your discomfort, right now.

You get used to your patterns of thinking and behaving and don't see yourself clearly. Habits blunt awareness and dampen alertness. You have undoubtedly gotten in your car and driven halfway to your office out of repetition when you really intended to go to the market. Your car virtually drove itself a distance before you remembered where you actually wanted to go.

It is so easy to get lost in your own head. News headlines are filled with very unhappy accidents that occur when people are detached.

A tragic case in point: It was a hectic Thursday morning last August. Five-month old Brayden was sleeping in the backseat of his mother's car in New York State when she arrived at her work just before 8:00 a.m. Brayden was to have spent the day, like every other weekday, at his child-care facility about a quarter of a mile from his mother's office.

The temperatures climbed that day into the 90's with high humidity. Experts estimate that the internal temperature of the car that day likely exceeded 130 degrees. Brayden was lifeless in his car seat when his mother arrived back at her car around 5:00 p.m.: his mother had forgotten to drop him off at the child-care facility. And his heartbreaking story isn't unique: Brayden was the 19th child to die in a hot car last summer in the US.

The number of such deaths has risen dramatically since the mid-1990s, totaling around 340 in the past ten years. Experts said the increase coincides with the practice of putting children in the back seat for safety purposes, where they are more easily forgotten. Is it any coincidence that the last ten years have also witnessed an exponential never-ending stream of information to the eyes and ears of already bombarded parents?

Life overlaps itself. You can accomplish more than ever before with the same 24 hours and at the same time lose track of what you really intend to achieve. Advances in technology and products accelerate your ability to accomplish tasks, yet increases your fear of falling behind.

Network Related Overload

The rise of computing networks has delocalized the workplace and work can be done almost all the time from everywhere. Do you recognize workplace transformation in this, the Information Age, is both a blessing and a curse?

If you believe this is our economic doomsday, you may have created an environment where you can't afford to stop working or worrying for even a moment. You fear that you could be replaced or displaced at a blink of an eye.

You may feel your job is no longer secure. Work may have lost much of its intrinsic pleasure for you. Almost everyone I speak to these days say that it is tough to enjoy work as much as they did previously. Everyone seems to be certain that the changing economy and new world order is to blame.

Familiar moments keep changing. You feel like you must chase every moment if you want to stay present and valuable. You fear every moment. Your struggle and frantic activity only aggravate the fundamental problem - feelings of fear.

Fear itself is not the problem that disables you. The *thoughts* that your mind attaches to your fear response is what detaches you from reality, consumes your mind, and dulls your senses.

Fear is actually just a physical sensation. The physical sensation tells your mind to act. If there is no outlet for action, fear gets tangled up in thoughts and spins around inside your head, veiling you from what is really going on around you.

When your fear sensation tells your mind to "fight or flee" and it is impossible for you to do either, a new predicament crops up. Psychologists and the authors of *Leadership Presence*, Belle Linda Halpern and Kathy Lubar call it the *inner critic.*

The inner critic is the voice inside your head that continually assesses your behavior. The voice inside your head screams at you until your mind eventually goes blank. The inner critic's messages are always the same, *you don't measure up, you are not good enough, this situation is too bad to change, you are a failure and everyone around you knows what a failure you are.*

During the 2005 commencement address at Stanford University, Steve Jobs, CEO of Apple Computer admonished, "Don't let the noise of other people's opinions drown out your own inner voice." But what if the disparaging voices are actually coming at you from inside your own head?

You may have come to think of the world as a hostile environment. Anger, guilt and shame pop up in your human psyche, whether the emotions are within your control or not. These are uncomfortable emotions. Your body produces unwanted fight or flight chemicals described above. So what do you do?

The only safe way to respond is to "detach" and create a "safety zone" between you and the rest of this dangerous world. Maybe you are completely unaware that you have become numb. You may be consumed by multi-tasking, distracted and stressed, not noticing that you have become "out of touch."

Recognize Your Authentic Self

The outside world can stop you temporarily – you are the only one who can do it permanently. You can change what you are and where you are by changing what is going on in your mind. Restore your vision with mastering skills of living fully present in the moment.

I did not recognize myself – the once radiant and courageous woman who pursued life with childlike zeal no longer appeared in my mirror. I was losing everything I cared about: my husband and my relationship with my children, my professional reputation, and my self-respect.

I had a huge awakening: my condition was, for the most part, self-imposed! My numbness, depression, and stress that I enforced on myself were an unnatural state of being. My emotions and the dullness of my senses were the warning signals that my current state was "abnormal;" out of sync with the way humans are wired. For humans, a natural state of being is joyful, at ease, vital, self-assured, healthy, loving, and passionate.

I have written this guide for people like you and me; those of us who have gotten "out of sync" with our natural flow of sensual energy. If this can happen to me, it can happen to anyone! My guide is for those of you that have put yourself at risk for ill health, accidents, poor relationships, and detachment from living that degrade your daily existence and may shorten your life.

There are life circumstances far more emotionally threatening, life altering situations such as a death of a loved one, severe illness, accidents, victimizing incidents of crime, financial ruin, natural disasters, etc., that require other means of professional support. Yet, even in these conditions, this guide can be a support tool to empower you to do more to influence your own recovery.

Vitality is not a finite element. There is no limited supply of vitality to be divided among all people on Earth. Imagine this world humming with millions of vital humans, taking responsibility for their own well-being, balancing their own energy flows. It's thrilling!

Moments to Capture from Chapter Two

As you master your ability to "feel," become self-aware by recognizing:

- Detachment in our present-day society is on the rise.

- Modern technology bombards you with information through multiple media devices in overlapping sequences, causing emotional fatigue.

- Habits blunt your awareness and dampen alertness to the point that you no longer see yourself clearly.

- Your *inner critic* is the voice of distraction and failure; don't listen to it!

- The way to restore your vision of reality is to live fully present in the moment and in sync with your natural flow of sensual energy.

CHAPTER THREE

Living Authentically

Introducing the Real You to the World

Becoming authentic means knowing and loving who you are; passionately experiencing the life you have created, knowing that a rich life happens now because there is no foolproof formula to securing a flawless future.

Authenticity is constructive self-interest. Constructive self-interest is about being yourself so completely that you can share yourself fully and beautifully with the world. Authenticity allows you to express the totality of who you are.

Your life is most fulfilling when you wake up to *who-you-really-are*. Self-knowledge, simply defined, is your ability to recognize what is important to you and what is not and to understand why you act as you do and why. Becoming self-aware, recognizing the way your mind works and of your patterns of thought and behavior allows you to influence the way you think and the behaviors you choose to have.

Are you asking yourself how you discover *who-you-really-are*? Susie Boyt, the British author of five books, *My Judy Garland Life, Only Human, The Characters of Love, The Last Hope of Girls* and *The Normal Man* praises a "selfish life":

Recently, I met the actress who was going to portray me in a radio adaption of my recent book, My Judy Garland Life. We met at a higgledy-piggledy Soho Café. She asked me to be my 'selfiest' self and she would be sort of a sponge and absorb me, the better to transmit me over the airwaves. Can you imagine!

I tried to show only my good sides, but with humility. I was like a greedy child who was seeking more attention than wise, but she didn't seem to mind. Afterward, when I heard the actual broadcast, she had observed me so acutely that she more closely resembled me than I do myself! She even had my mother near perfect; how did she do that?

There is so much talk of self-improvement, being faster, smaller, busier, and more rested; that the idea of celebrating what you are right now seems rather daring and radical. "Life's not worth a damn until you can say, hey world, I am what I am!"

Be Daring and Radical – Be Yourself

Now is a good time for you to become daring and radical!

Author, Mike Robbins, in his book, *Be Yourself, Everyone else Is Already Taken: The Power of Authenticity to Transform Your Life and Relationships* demonstrates how authenticity is about conquering fear or shame about being who you really are and accepting yourself, the intrinsic you, without a facade, pretentions, or fakery.

In his book, Robbins challenges you to "be bold" and offers five important attributes essential to living a bold life:

1. Be true to yourself
2. Live with passion
3. Step out
4. Lean on others
5. When you fall down, get up!

Do you at times, struggle with speaking with confidence, concerned about making mistakes? When you make mistakes, can you recover with sincerity, humbleness, and resilience? Are you able to take risks and go after what you really want, trusting that you deserve winning? Deep inside, do you know that your relationships, your work, and your life could be richer? Finding the real you brings a whole new sense of freedom.

Find the Real You – Do What You Want

What if right now, you commit for one week to do exactly what YOU want. So many times decisions in life are made because others tell you what you should do. What if you made all your decisions directly from your own gut? Would it trip an avalanche of disasters? It might. Or, would light be shining a little bit more brightly on humanity because of your choices? Either way, you discover the real you.

Are you familiar with the scientific research and writings of Candace B. Pert, PhD? Dr. Pert is the author of *Molecules of Emotion* and was featured in the film sensation, *What the #$*! Do We Know!?* Dr. Pert played herself in the film. She is credited with defining the science behind mind-body medicine.

Dr. Pert was part of the scientific team at Johns Hopkins University identifying endorphins, the "joy molecule." Endorphins are the body's own pain suppressors and "ecstasy inducers." Dr. Pert was seriously considered for an *Albert Lasker Medical Research Award*, sometimes referred to as America's "Nobels." As of 2008, there have been 75 Laskar Award recipients that have gone on to win Nobel Prizes in physiology and medicine.

Later, at Georgetown University School of Medicine, in the department of Physiology and Biophysics, she led a team to discover the gene sequence of the envelope protein surrounding HIV. This discovery led to the development of anti-retroviral medication, Peptide T (the "nickname" for a unique cell receptor blocker designed to block HIV from entering and infecting a cell).

During my medical research training at Georgetown University, Dr. Pert selected me as her research fellow. It was my great fortune to work side-by-side with Dr. Pert, acting as the clinical research manager for Peptide T, authoring Investigator IND submissions to the FDA for approval to conduct human clinical trials and to oversee those human clinical trials at St. Francis Hospital in San Francisco.

In the late 1980's and early 90's, Dr. Pert and I resonated instantly around our mutual belief that human emotions, the mind, and the soul, directly influence health outcomes. At that time, as it is today, science validates only what can be measured, thus proving its existence. Science theory upheld "measurement" as the very foundation of scientific method. Thus, intangibles such as "feelings" did not scientifically exist.

Scientific advancement often moves slowly. Boundary-breaking ideas are rarely welcome when first introduced in the scientific community. Scientists do not want to make mistakes. Their careers *depend* on not making mistakes. Imagine the opposition Dr. Pert and her delegation received when attempting to change the established paradigm of disease and human resistance.

Dr. Pert traveled across the world postulating a biochemical link between the body and the mind. She traced the pathway of emotions affecting a physical response in the body, in scientific terms. It was a new concept of the human organism as a communication network, empowering individuals to be accountable for their health by taking more control of their own lives.

I attended lectures with Dr. Pert. Her sense of humor, occasionally perverse, included toying with her audience. Sometimes, her teasing began even before she took the stage. She would arrive in the lecture theatre or convention hall at least 30 minutes before she was due to make her presentation. She sat in the audience in the second or third row and waited for the attendees to fill in around her.

Her presentations always brought in a mixed crowd, some medical doctors, some researchers, some new-age seekers, and some skeptics that all wanted to hear her theories of human emotion.

Confident that many of the attendees would not know her well enough to recognize her, Dr. Pert posed as a lecture attendee and asked very candid questions of others coming to hear her presentation.

She openly listened to attendees' assessment of what they expected to hear from her during the lecture and what they personally thought about her! Some called her "brilliant;" some called her a "quack." Others came to be "entertained" and others to find a "universal truth."

When the master of ceremonies took the stage and introduced Dr. Pert, she rose up from the audience and walked up onto the stage. After a brief period of gasps and giggles, Dr. Pert started her presentation. With the insight she received from her audience the attendees received exactly what they had come for. Dr. Pert is obviously open to feedback and secure with *who-she-really-is*.

Today, a couple of decades later, the concept of emotional influences on human behavior and health outcomes are well accepted and thoroughly documented by functional magnetic resonance imaging (fMRI), and various other scientifically accepted medical measurement techniques.

Dr. Pert demonstrated professional integrity in a quest for scientific truth, wherever the journey took her, regardless of the professional or personal price. Likewise, when I presented the concept for this book, I faced a similar type of scrutiny from my scientific peers. Several warned that I was risking my global health research career and my professional reputation by writing a "lifestyle" book. My desire to share my story overshadows the warnings of my peers. For me, living authentically is being a scientist and a dreamer. This is *who-I-really-am*.

Have you heard the adage, "If you are not happy without a lot of money, no amount of money will ever make you happy?" Do you believe it? I certainly do!

Every culture, in every country around the globe, throughout every generation, has pursued a happy life. You know money can't buy it. You see many people living with very little money, yet they remain happy.

Live a Rich Life

The richness of living is not material or financial wealth, it is an illusion that gratification comes from external sources. Material and financial wealth are no substitution for authentic engagement in life. How many miserable, angry, depressed or paranoid people of high net worth can you name? I imagine you can name quite a few.

What if it is not about the things you own, where you live, or even what happens to you? What if it is how you look at it? Is it all about your point of view?

My husband has jokingly said, "I have been rich and I have been poor, and rich is better." I believe this sentiment was originally expressed by Sophie Tucker (popular singer and comedian for half a century beginning around 1900). There is nothing wrong with wanting things. It is not wrong to want to do things and to go places. The whole point of pursuing an authentic sensual life is to experience life!

Abundance is the result of passionately and authentically partic-ipating in life. Enjoy the rewards, emotional and temporal. Regardless of what life throws your way, life itself is a magnificent opportunity if you experience it moment by moment.

Become part of the world around you. Not just recognizing extreme beauty, but noticing beauty in all things and the richness in the most simple of experiences.

Purposefully design your surroundings to please your senses. Use colors, textures, and elements from nature that feel uplifting to you. Everyone is different. Accessorize your home, your office, or car with bits and pieces that make you feel good. Spaces you spend time in can be rejuvenating or draining depending on the effect they have on your senses. Design and decorate your spaces to energize you. Treasure your uniqueness. Own it. Share it. If you can communicate the real you to your interior designer, you are 90% of the way there!

In order to embrace your authenticity, you must find peace with your "dark side," sometimes in psychology nicknamed, "your shadow self." Your shadow self consists of instincts and emotions that are, for the most part, suppressed in your unconscious. Your shadow self consists of what you feel is negative, malicious, wicked, or immoral about yourself.

Sometimes your shadow self acts like a mirror; the characteristics you most dislike in others are usually aspects of your shadow self that are hidden from view.

Why do you think I am asking you to reflect on your own shortcomings when I just instructed you to pay no attention to your inner critic? Because your "inner critic" and your "shadow self" are two separate things. Feminist activist, writer and lecturer, Gloria Steinem, in her bestselling book, *Revolution from Within: A Book of Self-Esteem,* states, "The truth will set you free. But first, it will piss you off!"

Before authentic personal change can occur, self-acceptance is required. You are not very good at fooling yourself if you acknowledge only the good in yourself. It is freeing to face your flaws as you bask in your own nobility. Self-acceptance is the right healthy emotional balance, being fully aware of your talents and your shortcomings.

View your life as a never-ending personal journey of transformation. Mistakes you make along the way become opportunities to change in the present moment. Failures teach you that you never get anywhere being "careful."

The final step to opening a space for your authenticity is removing negative influences of people in your life. As you read this sentence I am sure several faces came to mind. Let go of relationships that drain more of your energy than they give. I am not suggesting that you disown your mother-in-law. Just create boundaries for yourself that maintain your self-respect. Remember our discussion about constructive self-interest?

Authentic sensual living leads you to joy. Decide to live authentically – even if others think it is wrong, impossible, irresponsible, or worst of all, makes no money. I assure you, these concerns are myths; you are creating a rich life.

Moments to Capture from Chapter Three

In order to live authentically, accept:

- A rich life happens in the "now".

- Authenticity is constructive self-interest.

- Listening to yourself and make your own decisions.

- Material and financial wealth are no substitution for authentic engagement in life.

- Express yourself in your surroundings.

- Make peace with your "dark side."

- Authentic sensual living leads you to joy!

CHAPTER FOUR

Living Sensually

Firing on All Your Senses

The value of sensual enchantment is critically high in our increasingly disenchanted world. An emotional connection with your environment and others is a fundamental human need. To play the game of life, all channels must be tuned in.

Think of the word, **sensual**. Did an image of a woman come to your mind? Throughout time, men have been viewed as dominant and woman as sensually alluring. Sensuality is NOT merely sexuality. The word, "sensual" literally means, "of the senses." Sensuality is unisex, neither feminine nor masculine. It is the unseen energy that permeates all things. Every individual has been gifted with an array of senses in order to experience life and receive critical information.

Remove gender perceptions and "sensual" describes the essence of experiencing the full spectrum of emotions, using all five of your senses: sight, sound, smell, taste and touch. Consider adding your sixth sense, awareness and sense of knowing, intuition, a mysterious sense that has yet to be accurately measured or defined by science.

"Sense" comes from the Latin *sentire,* to feel. The Greek origin is *ousia,* the root of the word "essence," that which is one's own property. Your true self is defined by your unique senses. You are discovering who you really are through feeling your emotions through your senses. Exciting, isn't it?!

Taking pleasure in the senses is called "sensuality." Sensuality demands a response. Your response to your senses creates a relationship between you and your environment whether it is another person or a beautiful sunset.

At this point in time, many of you choose to suppress your sensuality, detach from your current surroundings and place barriers between yourself and those around you by focusing on the past, the future, and multi-tasking yourself into numbness, excessive worry or fear. Have you forgotten or repressed your senses? In other words, have you forgotten to "feel?"

You can experience each moment of your life through all your senses, often on multiple levels at the very same time. Yes, humans are able to create situations, environments and even thoughts that ignite your senses and enrich your life. You possess the quality of sensuality by virtue of being human. Authentic sensuality is honoring the primal instincts that make you truly part of nature.

Working much of my career in Africa, I observed wild animals in their natural surroundings. Animals in the wild, both predator and prey continually respond to life with all senses ignited. It is effortless for animals to harness the power of their senses, guiding their every action: taking in their surroundings, accessing their environment, trusting their instincts, acting upon the information that their senses provide.

Picture a female lioness tracking her prey, her ears forward and alert to detect the sound of rustling grass or the pounding of hooves in the distance, nostrils flared wide open to inhale the familiar scents of a pending meal, eyes keenly scanning the horizon and at the same time scrutinizing intricate details of her surroundings, paws feeling the ground beneath her with steadiness and agility, and finally, her innate "knowing," her understanding rhythm and cycles in the wild and how to play the survival game successfully.

In the wild, survival of the fittest depends on authentic sensual living. Your life may not always depend on your ability to experience life through your senses, but as you just read in the introduction of this book, on one particular summer day, my life did depend on it!

Feel the Sensations

Federico Fellini, one of the most illustrious and revered filmmakers of the 20th century was a model of authentic sensual living. Fellini insisted, "You have to live spherically, experiencing life from many directions all at once. Never lose your childlike wonder and wild imagination."

Fellini's films portrayed his personal vision of society; his unique combination of sensual memories, dreams, fantasies and desires. Fellini's characters are multi-dimensional and do bizarre things in ordinary situations, the types of things that you always wished you could do! In Fellini's film *La Dolce Vita*, the lead character, Marcello, an Italian journalist, lives the life men fantasize about; soliciting telephone numbers from beautiful bikini clad women sunbathing on a roof top as he passes by overhead in a helicopter. In another scene in the film, Marcello is dipping and dancing with a ravishing film star named Sylvia in Fontana di Trevi. This fountain scene, filmed in 1960 remains one of the most sensual moments in film history.

Touch is the sense we associate mostly with sensuality. Your receptor for touch is the largest organ of your body, your skin. While still in your mother's womb, you were experiencing your sense of touch. At the moment of your birth, your skin touched your mother's skin and you responded to her sweet caress. Your first human relationship was defined by touch. Sight, sound, taste and smell are also primitive sense states; you continued developing these senses as you matured. As an adult, you can continue developing all of these senses. It is never too late!

Your mind is programmed to receive images, make interpretations and draw conclusions. Pictures archived in your mind provides context for your world. Not even blindness veils the images your mind can "see" and interpret. Sight is a mechanism for your mind to gather information. Color dominates visual data collection. Even without varied color hues, images registered only in shades of grey provide emotional data for your mind to interpret.

Gloucester, a lead character in one of Shakespeare's famous tragedies, *King Lear,* suffered having his eyes gouged out by his enemies. Gloucester roamed the world a blind and dispirited man. Time passed and Gloucester endured. He began to "see" the truth of things. King Lear says to Gloucester, "You have no eyes, yet you see how this world goes," and Gloucester replied, "I see it feelingly." He learned to see the world through all his other senses and through the eyes of others. Gloucester, equipped with perfect introspective vision, claimed, "I stumbled when I saw, so great is my ability now to see."

Smell, along with touch, is our most primitive sense; in fact, it is the most dominant sense for many mammals. Your sense of smell is stuffed with instinctive associations, originating ages ago. Breathing in and out through your nose triggers the sense of smell constantly, allowing you to sample scents around you effortlessly by simply being alive.

Sense of smell varies from person-to-person; what smells good to you may not smell good to another. Your brain is capable of distinguishing among thousands of specific odors. Your olfactory bulbs, the tiny organs that detect scents, are directly connected to the emotion center of your brain, the limbic system. That is exactly why aromas, both good and bad, elicit strong emotional responses.

Scents unlock emotions. Think about the last time you put your nose near a bouquet of flowers; remember how the scent raised your spirits for a moment. Did a spontaneous smile brighten your face? Did you briefly close your eyes to isolate and enhance the fragrance you enjoyed? See how your emotions are stirred by your memory of the scent of flowers?

Aromatic oils and herbs have been used for millennia, as aphrodisiacs and seductive potions. The Egyptians used scents for healing and to induce pleasant dreams. Likewise, the Greeks used various scented oils as antidepressants, sleep aids, and aphrodisiacs.

Modern research demonstrates how smells influence mood, evoke emotions, counteract stress and enrich our living environment. Activating your sense of smell and evoking emotion markets products ranging from body lotion to toilet bowel cleaner.

Colors trigger feelings. Colors are powerful attractors. White, for example, is powerful in situations of confrontation because it disarms your rival. The Pope wears white. Gandhi wore white. Joan of Arc wore white boldly into battle. Leading her troops into combat, there was no mistaking the commander leading the charge! She appeared invincible.

Vivid colors exude strength. Pastels convey gentleness or peace. Background colors of nature, such as greens, blues, and shades of brown radiate tranquility. Black and grays are camouflage colors, much like a frame around a picture, focusing what is inside.

Sound has a direct pathway to your emotional responses. Feelings attach to rhythms, tones, pitches, volume, and especially to musical lyrics.

In the womb, a fetus hears sounds that provide some of the first interactions she has with the inside and outside world. Her inside world is full of her mother's sounds: her heartbeat, digestion, and breathing sounds. The muffled sounds of the outside world can evoke responses in the womb either by startling the fetus and soothing her.

Sounds provide a shortcut to communication such as warning sirens, the bell at the start of a horse race, or your father's whistle to return home for dinner when you were a child.

Your voice is a powerful multifaceted instrument. Pitch, volume, cadence, style all send distinct messages that influence the interpretation of your words. The sound that you communicate is a language far beyond the words you say.

Sojourner Truth, a slave toward the end of the Civil War used her voice to save her own life and eventually buy her own freedom. She was walking to her home one night when she was confronted by an angry mob. Sojourner had no time to run and no place to hide.

Sojourner did a startling and unexpected thing: she walked down the center of the street, in full view of the approaching mob and began singing at the top of her voice. The men in the mob were stunned! They were not prepared to defend themselves against a song.

The mob lowered their sticks and knives and listened. Sojourner continued to sing. The mob softened. One mobster encouraged her to keep singing, saying, "Sing more Sister, sing more." She was allowed to pass, unharmed.

Appetite and taste are barometers of your well-being. Having a "healthy appetite" might have been an endearing phrase that your grandmother used to describe your eating habits as an adolescent. Moreover, she was giving you a medical diagnosis. Stress and illness suppress appetite. Taste, or the lack of it, drives consumption of food. When you say, "nothing tastes good," you are probably describing your emotional or physical state of being, not your body's need for nourishment.

Dr. David Frawley, author of Ayurvedic Healing: A Comprehensive Guide says, "Emotions have the same effect as foods or herbs of the same energetic quality. Anger can damage your liver as much as alcoholism." So herbs and diet are not enough if the taste of the mind has not changed.

Food affects your mind as well as your body. There are basically three categories of emotional foods: there are foods that dull your mind, slow your systems down; there are foods that arouse energy production, speed up your metabolism and stimulate your mind; and there are foods that produce clarity, harmony and balance in your mind and your body functions.

Dylan's Candy Bar purveys bulk candy and is situated across from Bloomingdales in Manhattan. During the current economic recession, business is "sweet" you might say! Storeowners like Dylan's, producers of Tootsie Rolls and Gummy Bears, and industry experts say, "As unemployment rises in Manhattan, adults in the city are consuming growing volumes of candy!"

Candy sales surges are widespread. In Chicago, at the shop Candyality, sales are up 80% over the same time last year. The store-owner struggles to keep up with demand on some brands of candy. In San Francisco, the same is true at the Candy Store. Customers tell the storeowner that they set money aside specifically to buy candy; that candy is a line item in their personal budgets!

Market researchers have theories about why this is. Sugar can lift your spirits for brief periods of time. A clinical study showed chocolate to be as effective as Prozac for short-term mood reversal. Candy is nostalgic, it reminds us of a kinder time in your early youth when parents looked after all your worldly needs. Candy is also relatively low-priced. Have you noticed that most all people in a candy store are happy? During tougher times, people like to be around other happy people, it is somehow infectious. Enjoying the taste of candy makes people feel a little less deprived.

A vibrant diet includes all three categories of emotional foods! Eat passionately; spice up your life and soothe your senses by experiencing a plethora of flavors. Be adventurous; taste your way through life and connect with your feelings that a variety of flavors stir up.

Every moment of every day, your body is a gigantic thermometer; sensing internal and external temperature. I am certain you rarely think about this constant physical process going on unless you are triggered to regulate temperature in some particular way.

Reflect on the emotions you feel when a server at an upscale Japanese restaurant hands you a steamy warm towel prior to your meal. Do you exhale with pleasure and do start to salivate over the thought of the delicious meal to come?

Is there anything more welcoming about the ice-cold towel you put on your face when coming out of a blistering hot sauna or off the playing field during a sultry summer tennis match? When you have sore muscles or an injury, an ice pack and or a heating pad feels awfully soothing.

Temperature charms your life when you least expect it. A sense of peace overcomes you when you pull a fresh shirt from the dryer and hold it to your face; the clean scent and warmth of the fabric provokes a grateful grin. Step off an airplane in mid-January into a tropical locale. The tropic heat and humidity instantly tell you that you are a world away from a Minnesota winter.

Step into a cool wine cellar and recognize the sweet smell of fruit as well as the inviting temperature begging you to linger and inspect the wine bottles. Add ice cubes to your beverage at the pool. Make a mug of hot tea or coffee to get you started on a chilly morning. So much of what we do to give ourselves comfort is all about adjusting temperature.

Emotional sensitivity springs forth from your sixth sense – your intuition. The intangible love and connection you have for the human race; compassion, empathy, moral and ethical consciousness stem from your intuitive nature.

Innately, heroes dash into burning buildings or dive into frigid waters, risking their own existence to protect a fellow human being, even a stranger. These valiant actions, driven solely from deep feelings (emotions) instruct the brain instantly how to respond.

Oscar winner and leading lady of stage and screen, Meryl Streep claims, "*It is the greatest gift of human beings that we have this power of empathy. We can all feel like Elliott when E.T. died. We can all cry for each other. We can all sense a mysterious connection to each other. And that's good. If there's hope for the future of us all, it lies in that. When I'm drawn out of my own life into someone else's life, suddenly, I myself feel more alive!*"

Although almost impossible to measure or define, there are characteristics of intuition you have all felt. The list below contains a few that come to mind for me:

- As you contemplate a course of action, you feel a sense of peace.
- An idea or thought repeatedly comes to your mind and you can't ignore the promptings you feel.

- As you set your sights on a goal, a pathway and new opportunities unfold almost effortlessly, enabling you to move ahead rapidly.
- Conversely, when a course does not "feel right" obstacles and barriers appear frequently, impeding progress toward the goal and causing fatigue.
- In times of need, your courage, strength and clear thinking magnifies to match the situation and you spring into action without hesitation.
- Gratitude fills your heart and you feel like you are exactly where you should be at this time of your life.

I am certain that you can add more symptoms of intuition to this list from your own experiences. Suffice it to say, the sixth sense exists beyond our current ability to measure.

You share the same primal urges for food, sleep, self-preservation, and sex drive with all animal life on this planet. Primal urges are driven by your senses. Only you, and other humans, can regulate these urges consciously. The power you have to manage your primal urges, suppressing and igniting them, frees you to experience higher levels of consciousness and live "richer" in each moment.

Moments to Capture from Chapter Four

In order to live sensually, accept:

- The word, "sensual" literally means, "of the senses." It is the unseen energy that permeates all things. Every individual has been gifted with an array of senses in order to experience life and receive critical information.

- Taking pleasure in the senses is called "sensuality." Sensuality demands a response. Your response to your senses creates a relationship between you and your environment.

- You can experience each moment of your life through all your senses, often on multiple levels at the very same time.

"Sensuality" describes the essence of experiencing the full spectrum of emotions using all six of your senses: sight, sound, smell, taste, touch and intuition.

CHAPTER FIVE

Exploring the Science of Sensuality

Your Emotions Control Your Mind

As a scientist, I am compelled to write a chapter validating the *science of sensuality*. I promise to make this chapter brief for those of you who opted out of science-related courses once you fulfilled your general education requirements! The scientific thesis is as follows:

Humans have the capability to experience life moment to moment with all their senses ignited, in as much as several or all of their senses may be stimulated at the same time, providing for a richly satisfying holistic experience.

How does your brain code and analyze sensory information and use that information to shape your perception of the world? Neuroscientists argue that the mind and the body are bound together and who you are depends very much on the experiences that are regulated by your sensory systems.

Multi-sensory Input

In nature, most all species must have multiple sensory channels to monitor their environment and to guide their actions in order to thrive and reproduce. You, like most living creatures, have many sources of sensory input that can operate simultaneously or substitute for another when necessary; such as in darkness, your sense of hearing and touch can compensate for your inability to see.

You might say that simultaneous sensory channels multiply your world-view because each modality is tuned to a different form of energy, each contributing a unique perceptual experience. The sound of the waves crashing on a rocky shoreline is nothing like the taste of a hot buttery croissant; the sight of a rainbow is nothing like the rough texture of sand paper. The perception of sour is specific to taste. The perception of an itch is limited to feel. The perceptions of pitch and volume are exclusive to hearing, even though, if you are incredibly sensitive, you can feel the changes in vibration various sounds make.

All of your senses are distinctly different. Yet, you are continually using your senses in perfect harmony, quite effortlessly. Quality of life is enhanced by integration of sensory inputs. Integrated sensory input creates rich experiences. Drs. Barry Stein and Alex Meredith, in their book, "*The Merging of the Senses,*" describe aroma and texture as independent cues associated with food that contribute characteristics to your sense of taste. Change either of those two factors and food will taste different.

Multi-sensory integration allows you tremendous response flexibility. The presence of one sensory stimulus alters the presence of another sensory input, providing context. Consider the effects of a good ventriloquist. Watching the movement of a devilishly charming puppet, dressed in his top hat and monocle, captivates you. The puppet's eyes, lips, head, and hands seem "alive" with exaggerated movement.

The ventriloquist is perfectly still when speaking, yet positioned very close to the puppet.

Generally, visual input carries the strongest energy. The ventriloquist's trick is to direct your full attention to the puppet. Then it is up to you, the perceiver, to interpret the interaction among the various sensory inputs.

Though visual input is high energy, your reaction to auditory stimulus is faster by approximately 40 - 60 milliseconds, due to your anatomy. The processing time of your retina in your eye is slightly slower compared to your processing mechanisms of your middle ear. A gunshot will send racers off the mark quicker than a starter waving a flag.

However, if more than one stimulus is synchronized in such a way that the sensory inputs are sent to the brain at the same time, your reaction time becomes significantly shorter! Consider the Kentucky Derby. Horses bolt out of racing gates faster when a combination of sensory signals simultaneously set them off; the shrill blaring sound of the bell, gates bursting open and swift snap of the jockeys' crop.

Scientific investigators may not agree on the exact mechanisms by which it occurs, but most agree, bi- or multi-sensory stimuli speed up your reactions.

Anatomy and Perception

Human sensory organs: eyes, ears, mouth, and skin continually encounter stimuli and the sensory channel process begins. Visual, auditory, and somatosensory (pertaining to sensations received in the skin and deep tissues and organs) stimuli travel to neuro-junctions at the neuron level. Neurons are the smallest nerve cells; among any of the conducting cells of the nervous system. Neurons consist of a cell body containing the nucleus and its surrounding cytoplasm, the axon and dendrites.

Think of neurons as tiny tributaries that lead to mountain streams that feed into a larger river. The visual tributary meets the auditory and somatosensory tributary and the stimuli integrate as it moves toward the mid-brain for processing. Different types of stimuli are processed in various portions of the midbrain, having very different impacts on behavior and perception, yet all stimuli travel similar neuro pathways.

Modern medical technology provides tools to understand these complex sensory mechanisms and the connection between external sensory input and your mind's processing and decision-making mechanisms. Positron emission tomography (PET) scanning (a cross-sectional image of a metabolic process in a human body produced by the positive electrical impulse emitted from the proton of human molecules in which the movements of fluids such as blood and spinal fluid are detectable) and functional magnetic resonance imaging (fMRI) (a form of magnetic resonance imaging of the brain that registers blood flow to functioning areas of the brain; indicating comparative changes in levels of brain activity) display the anatomical and physiological effects, such as increased blood flow to particular brain regions upon sensory stimulation, sight, sound, touch, smell, and even emotional responses you generate from your perception of the stimuli.

This process of integration is of great importance to survival and explains the extraordinary evolutionary process that many scientists believe occurred in the nervous systems of animals as diverse as fish, reptiles, birds, and mammals, including you. Certain species require acutely different sensory priorities to survive.

Intersection of Perception

Your environment contains an incessantly shifting kaleidoscope of perceivable events. Stimuli occur at various times and proximities, events occur outside your control and it is your responsibility to comprehend sensory input and create perceptual order of it all. You determine your perceptional map, so to speak.

The process is only successful when you can determine which stimuli are related to each other and which are not. This relationship is based on significance of the sensory signal. The significance is assigned by your mind, partially by genetics (intrinsic circuitry of the brain), partially by experience, and partially by chemical effects (which is not a topic we will discuss in this book, yet is part of the overall effect).

As described above, as part of nature's adaptive process, sensory significance can be altered. Not only is it an evolutionary process for survival, many voluntary external factors can enhance or impede sensory inputs. Imagine a domestic cat lazily walking among bushes in a garden. There is a bird chirping a song, hidden in the leaves of a bush. The cat continues to walk, unaffected by the song of the bird. The bird stops chirping and flies gently to a lower branch, no longer hidden by leaves. Again, the cat continues to stroll by the bush. The bird begins to chirp its familiar song. This time, the cat stops, crouches, and immediately pounces at the bird. Stimuli of both sight and sound reached a significant level for affect.

External affects interrupt sensory channel effects, often by intention. To demonstrate this point, Dr. Barry Stein set up an experiment by designing a three-sided box. He equipped the box with seven sets of auditory speakers, LED lights, and a small food tray below. The set of speakers and lights represented multisensory stimuli and the food was the reward. Cats were selected as the research subjects. Cats are not well known for their obedience, but they respond well to edible rewards. Dr. Stein compared the cats' ability to distinguish between auditory and visual stimuli on command by varying the reward in a particular pattern. The cats were conditioned to move toward the light when food appeared as they approached close to the source. Then the pattern was reversed and the cats were conditioned to move toward the sound to receive the reward. The third trial tested the cats' responses to a light going on in one location and the sound in another. The cats quickly learned to ignore one or the other sensory stimulus in order to consistently receive the reward.

In an unsophisticated, yet scientifically mysterious way, you condition yourself to become unresponsive to external stimuli and ignore sensory input provided in your environment. Pause in your reading for a moment and pay attention to everything else around you: is there a scene outside your window, a draft that makes you feel chilly, a sunbeam that warms you, a smell of bread baking that makes you hungry, or the sound of traffic?

Psychology of Perception

Scientific contributions to the "science of the mind" and multisensory integration are varied and come from several disciplines: neurology, neuroscience, philosophy, and psychology. Psychology, however, has the firmest hold on the "study" of human perception.

Historically, identifying qualities of subjective experiences produced by each of the senses and their ability to reflect events accurately in the real world has been illuminated in psychiatric, psychological, and psychosocial studies.

What are emotions? Why do you "feel?" Feelings are the expression of emotion. All emotions have a feeling component, a sensory component, a thinking component, and an action component. Dr. Martin Seligman, in his book, "*Authentic Happiness*," argues that feelings are part of an evolutionary process, essential to survival as a protection when quick and decisive action is required: fight, flight or conserve. Your sensory component is the integration of your senses; of sight, sound, touch, smell, and taste giving you information, for defense, safety, and comfort. Your feelings tell your mind what to think. Your thoughts guide your actions. The entire cycle begins with your feelings and culminates in your behavior. The way you present yourself to the world is actually an emotional mirror. Happiness and contentment really do originate deep within your emotional self.

Dr. Seligman also postulates that the barrier to raising your level of happiness is what he has labeled, "the hedonic treadmill." When on the hedonic treadmill, you swiftly and inevitably *adapt to good things by taking them for granted.* As you accumulate more material possessions and accomplishments, your expectations rise. It becomes an endless vicious circle. The more good things that happen to you in your life the less precious positive experiences seem. If this principle were not true, the people experiencing more fortunate events in life would generally be more joyful than those experiencing more disappointing events. But the less fortunate, for the most part, are as content and happy than those blessed with success and positive experiences. The inverse is not true. You don't adapt to bad events in your life as readily.

Your emotional response to stimuli is very similar to your physiological response. First of all, genetics determine the set range of your innate emotional capacity. Second, the circumstances you live in, and finally, the voluntary choices you make. In order to understand the authentic you, consider your genetic temperament and identify your unique core values, based on your perception of life. There are no wrong conclusions. Voluntarily take responsibility for your happiness by designing a rich and stimulating environment to live each day of your life.

Aesthetics of Perception

Context, rather than any particular stimulus, determines response and behavior. Even the simplest behavior requires sensory integration on the cellular level. In the study of your sensory system, aesthetics is the synthesis of accepting sensory input, processing sensations based on your own perceptual map and producing a thought and/or action.

What is beauty: a sight, a sound, a taste, a feeling, some combination of all of these? What characteristics satisfy the definition for beautiful? Beauty is not a trait that is inherent to any object. According to David Hume, the Scottish philosopher, it is an attribute of the "mind, which contemplates them." Beauty is in the eye of the beholder. The beholder is you!

Moments to Capture from Chapter Five

Thesis for the *Science of Sensuality:*

"Humans have the capability to experience life moment to moment with all their senses ignited, in as much as several or all of their senses may be stimulated at the same time, providing for a richly satisfying holistic experience."

- In nature, most all species must have multiple sensory channels to monitor their environment and to guide their actions in order to thrive and reproduce.

- Each sensory modality: sight, sound, touch, taste, and smell are tuned to a different form of energy, each contributing a unique perceptual experience.

- Multi-sensory integration allows you tremendous response flexibility. The presence of one sensory stimulus alters the presence of another sensory input, providing context.

- Medical imaging devices such PET scans and fMRI capture physiological effects such as increased blood flow to particular brain regions upon sensory stimulation, sight, sound, touch, smell, and even emotional responses generated from perception of stimuli.

- As part of nature's adaptive process, sensory significance can be altered. Not only is it an evolutionary process for survival, many voluntary external factors can enhance or impede sensory inputs.

- All emotions have a feeling component, a sensory compo- nent, a thinking component, and an action component.

- Aesthetics is the synthesis of accepting sensory input, processing sensations based on an individual's perceptual map and producing a thought and/or action.

CHAPTER SIX

Radiantly Authentic and Sensual

You Already Have Everything You Need

Passion for authentic sensual living translates into passion for life. As you authentically experience life with all your senses, living in the present, you see its beauty in its full splendor.

The key to harnessing the power of authenticity and sensuality is to allow your **emotions** to reign and your mind to serve. Your senses are directly linked to emotions and your mind is the software that interprets the input, makes decisions based on the input and directs physical responses. You respond authentically, being *who-you-really-are*, when you shift from your mind to your heart.

Living an authentic sensual life means living fully in the present; experiencing every moment in its richness. Moments of our lives are attached to a spectrum of emotions, pleasurable and painful; joyful and stressful, playful and intense; all are rich experiences. However, your life can become "cluttered" if you are overly focused on the past or future instead of on the present. Reality is only in the present. The only moment that exists is the moment we are in.

Physical and Emotional Vitality

Authentic sensual radiance is the flow of sensual energy; it is physical and emotional vitality. Some people, both women and men, seem to be born with this type of radiance. Sensual radiance seems like a mysterious quality, yet it is not really mysterious at all. You have seen it run in families, but that does not mean that this type of radiance is genetic.

Authentic sensual radiance requires all your senses to be ignited. Experiencing life through your senses sparks a myriad of emotions, often at a subconscious level, far below the level of your conscious mind's functions. Emotions drive your decision-making mechanisms, conscious and subconscious.

You have asked yourself sometimes why some men and women who are not overly attractive draw attention and success naturally. *You have this innate quality.* You can evoke it. The radiant energy you evoke that attracts others is your "aliveness." You experience sensual radiance in your life from time to time. Remember what it felt like when you were in the flow, really "on your game?" Would you like to feel in the flow most of the time?

Igniting your senses will become your way of life as you feel the pleasure of sensually balanced living. Your sense of sight, touch, sound, smell, taste, and intuition are designed to give you the right information for your mind to calibrate your choices to maintain your health and vitality.

Seeking Perfect Balance

Sensual radiance begins with the *balance of health.* Your body is a network of interconnected systems that are impacted by stimuli, both internally and externally. Your body systems must be in balance in order to perform at the highest functioning level. Balanced or imbalanced health can occur at any age. Natural aging takes place when cells are damaged at the molecular level. Our lifestyle, state of health, and physiological response to stressors influence how effectively our bodies maintain balance.

The discussion of "free radicals" and other biophysical responses to stressors are not necessary to discuss in the context of this book, but I encourage you to pursue further examination of this topic as your scientific interests dictate.

In the fall of 2005 I was invited to Deauville, France to offer a presentation at a global economic forum. I was asked to speak on the topic of balancing your health.

I started by explaining that the practice of medicine is an art and a science of maintaining and restoring the perfect balance of health. *Science* of medicine is based on a foundation of what can be measured. *Art* of medicine is that which has not yet been measurably defined, but can predictably affect health.

As a young science student, I was taught that even the smallest molecules in our bodies strictly follow the laws of physiology and biophysics. It was fascinating to observe human cells function. Healthy cell behavior is so predictable! I began to understand how laws of biophysics existed, long before scientists determined how to measure them.

Our health and emotional well-being depends on a delicate balance of systems, from the smallest molecules in our bodies to balancing our common global environment.

At the same conference, Cherie Booth Blair, wife of ex-British Prime Minister, Tony Blair was also speaking. She was assigned the topic of balancing work and family. As a practicing attorney, a mother of four, and wife to a British PM, she had some humorous stories and great wisdom for balancing your life.

At the luncheon, following the morning presentations, we determined that we had really been assigned the same topic: **balancing energy**, whether it was bio-chemicals in your body, climate change on planet Earth, children's homework schedule, or your social calendar.

All of these systems are interrelated and a healthy world begins with healthy balanced people.

Dr. Phil Neurenberger, in his book *The Quest for Personal Power: Transforming Stress into Strength,* states that stress is a state of autonomic imbalance, either arousal or inhibition, or a complex unbalanced interaction of the two. Stress is created in your mind. The intended function of stress is a message from your mind warning your body that there is present danger and emergency action may be required

Scientific research shows the right combinations of diet, physical activity, and techniques of personal mastery all affect your metabolism. In scientific terms, *metabolism* is the physical process of creating energy to power you as a human machine. Just like tuning your engine, changing your oil, and replacing worn tires increase the function, safety and efficiency of your vehicle, giving proper attention to your physical and emotional maintenance tunes your body's metabolism. Functioning with a well-tuned metabolism radiates energy. Your sensual radiance makes you feel alive and is alluring to others!

You can recognize people with sensual radiance by the sparkle in their eyes, the energy in their walk, their sense of wonder about the world around them, inclination to adventure, openness to outcome, self-assurance and their passionate nature.

Breathing is at the core of our internal flow of energy and creates a bridge between the mind and the body. This interaction occurs whether you are paying attention to it or not. You experience the flow of energy and the interruption of this flow throughout the course of your day. A "breathtaking" experience comes when a wave of emotion causes you to inhale deeply and hold your breath. When frightened, you nearly stop breathing. You sigh with emotional relief with a long exhale.

Physical activity, any type of exercise that you enjoy and consistently participate in, will stimulate your metabolism and enhance your sensual radiance. All physical activity will increase blood circulation throughout your body, supplying necessary nutrients to your organs, muscles, and glands, improving metabolic cell function, and facilitating efficient waste elimination. Sufficient blood supply to the brain heightens the acuity of all your senses. Strong bones and flexible muscles maintain your agility and balance. Sensual pleasures are magnified as you develop your body's consciousness.

World-champion female bodybuilder, Olympic athlete and best-selling author, Gayle Olinekova illustrates in her book, *The Sensuality of Strength* that true gentleness comes from strength. She testifies that your body can transmit an abundance of continually renewable pleasures – if you allow it to do so. She claims you don't have to be an Olympic athlete to have the benefits of improved fitness and the vitality that increased strength can give. Gayle emphasizes, "Just once in your life, let it be now." It is the time for you to care for your body and enjoy the values of fitness and health:

"Death is the currency that makes life valuable and abundant. Death makes the reality of our birth and living even more wonderful. If we lived forever, would time be as precious? If there were no destruction, would creation still be a miracle to us? Even on the most mundane level, this holds true."

Gayle speaks with wisdom. Why would you wait? Why would you waste a day, an hour or a moment when your moments are in finite supply?

Moments to Capture from Chapter Six

Passion for authentic sensual living translates into passion for life.

- The key to harnessing the power of authenticity and sensuality is to allow your emotions to reign and your mind to serve.

- Living an authentic sensual life is living fully in the present; experiencing every moment in its richness.

- Sensual radiance begins with the balance of health.

CHAPTER SEVEN

Sensually Authentic and Sexual

A Case Against Faking Orgasms

The world could use a little more pleasure and playfulness. Play balances life's complexities.

As Dr. Halpern's research demonstrates in the afterword of this book, human pleasure is a good, positive, and desirable thing. Research shows pleasure, including sexual pleasure, eases stress, calms nerves and balances emotional energy. Possibly a divine gift!

Sexual authenticity is your ability to experience *who-you-really-are* most fully; the ability to transfer sensually radiant energy to your lover; and to receive your lover's full authentic expression in return. Sexual authenticity is giving AND receiving with complete abandon. Sexual authenticity is healthy and is essential to living a rich life.

Sensuality is a life-long gift you give to yourself. Sexual attractiveness is based on radiance and vitality, not merely on youthfulness and external good looks. Sexual energy suppressed can be a disease risk factor for both physical and emotional health. An inability to form authentic relationships with one's self and with others is at the core of many psychological disorders.

Authentic sensuality and radiance draws out a similar radiance in other people. Sexual vitality is the magnet. The most sensual relationship is with a lover that knows *who-he-really-is* and has authentic self-love. The sure way to attract a sensually authentic lover is to be radiant and receptive when you meet.

Sexual authenticity is not *goal directed*. You transfer energy back and forth between you and your lover and the surge of energy you feel vitalizes your being. If you have been in your relationship for a while and feel you have lost some mystery and passion, rediscover your lover through intentionally engaging all your senses: smell him, lick him, touch him lightly in a different place, listen to the sound of his breathing, and watch him respond.

Power of Sexual Energy

Women's breasts are a source of hidden power. There are many examples, but here are (appropriately enough!) two of them: The Amazons, a matriarchal tribe historically believed to have existed as long ago as sixth century BC, were trained in the arts of war at a very young age. Stories of beautiful, yet bloodthirsty bands of Amazon women who fought with their breasts exposed are linked with the perception of the Amazonians as fearsome warriors. They used their bodies as a weapon against their enemies. As a charging gang of warriors, these fiery women stopped attackers in their tracks with the sight of their exposed female forms. Their breasts sent a powerful message. Many centuries later, the legends of Amazon warriors continue.

India, 1971: a group of social protesters, both men and women marched a street in Mumbai, formerly Bombay. Their march led them into the clutches of a large and angry opposing throng, armed with iron rods and knives. The social protesters were outnumbered. The situation was dire.

Immediately, acting purely on intuition, the women of the social protesting group surrounded their male colleagues. Shoulder to shoulder these women faced the angry crowd, challenging them only with their feminine presence: chests raised, skirts waving softly around their forms; creating a barrier before the hostile crowd of men. The men advanced a few steps, faltered, and then slowly backed away, allowing the protestors to proceed with their march.

I am not suggesting that you head to your office in the morning topless, however, I encourage you, both men and women, to own your uniquely male or female sensually radiant power and authentically portray a model of the best your gender has to offer. I promise you, sexual energy is an untapped resource. Manage sexual energy responsibly and you command most all situations.

Think of the performers and politicians who have owned and managed their sexual energy responsibly: Sean Connery, Bono, and Barrack Obama!

Why Fake "It" When You Can Have the Real Thing?

Sexual intercourse is an exchange of energy that has the potential of uniting you with another human being to create new life. However, the closeness, intimacy and pleasure of caressing and being caressed by someone you care about and respect can be as rewarding as the orgasmic "spasm" itself.

Metaphorically at least, it is possible for you to have marvelous orgasmic experiences without having sex at all. Athletes, artists, adventurers, and possibly you yourself have experienced the "bliss of creation" aside from sexual intercourse, during work or while deeply engrossed in recreational or artistic pursuits. Time spent with family and friends often rise to levels of heavenly happiness because these rich relationships are profoundly rewarding.

The orgasmic process (with or without sex) is relatively simple. Stimulation occurs and the signal is sent to your brain that pleasure is on the way. Your brain, an adherent of pleasure, responds through the nervous system, which increases blood flow and muscle tension. Your heart rate increases, blood pressure rises causing a "flushed" feeling and there is no better physical feeling in the whole world.

In that moment of "orgasmic bliss" (again, with or without sex) time stands still. No one feels stress, for there is only that moment, completely consuming and joyful. Ah – now you remember what an orgasm feels like! Why fake it?

Sexual authenticity is based in trust. Honesty, trustworthiness and respect are absolute essential prerequisites for sex, on a first encounter or after 30 years of marriage. A solid sense of self is the foundation for your lifelong sexual satisfaction. Bringing the real you, authentic and fully present, to your intimate encounters permits you to give and receive energy in an endless flow. As I asked before, why fake it?!

Essential Tool Box

I have two words of advice for you as you grow more sexually authentic and sensual – *Have fun!*

Sex is about delight, desire, intimacy, connection, and caring. If you are hung up on technique, you are missing the point.

Surrender yourself to the moment, become mindless, relax, touch, give and receive affection, and be aware of the natural ways your body and mind become aroused by playfully connecting with another person.

In this chapter, I give you general approaches to igniting your sexual self. I help you set the stage and suggest a few essentials to get you on track. The journey is yours. There are volumes of books and videos available specifically to instruct your sexual play. I persuade you to conduct your own exploration and encourage you to build your tool chest with items that excite you. Here are a few of my favorites!

Integrate the environment and create atmosphere. Variety adds spice to the mix. Add music, contrasting lighting with candles or fireplace, scent the air with candles or fragrant bamboo reeds, place a flower on the nightstand, and fill a tub with warm water. Add oil or soft bubbles. Be with your partner outdoors on a fluffy blanket.

Try something new. Break out of your old patterns. Add a new "twist" in your familiar sexual routine. Make a game of it, tell a story to each other and become the characters, play out a secret fantasy by pretending to be on a date, or even enact how it might have been when you first met. Have you ever tried a form of "phone sex" with your partner? It doesn't have to include self-stimulation, if that is not comfortable for you. Let your imagination loose.

Build a boudoir wardrobe. Build your specialized unique wardrobe of lingerie, satin scarves, feathers, leather chaps, and an array of amusing pieces. Be "alluring." Act "naughty." Enfold yourself in many layers for your partner to unwrap like a special gift. Role play. Enact your wildest fantasy as a pirate and princess, doctor and patient, or bride and groom (clad only in a wedding veil and garter for her and bow tie for him).

Ensure comfort. Place a fresh glass of water, tissues, a few cushy pillows, the right-size condom, breath mist, and a high quality water-based lubricant within reach. Lubricant is a necessity; not an accessory. Applying the right amount of water-based lubricant at the right times in the right places amplifies pleasurable sensations. Lubricant prevents irritation from back-and-forth motion and encourages natural lubrication to increase, while at the same time releasing additional pleasure hormones. Research has shown that irritated tissues increase microbe transmission. Healthy tissues ensure maximum pleasure and long-term well-being. Water-based lubricants are not the right consistency for body massage. Oils and lotions for massage are not intended for internal uses. Have both sacred fluids on hand. (Pack similar items in your backpack for outdoor adventures!)

Adhere to wise health practices. Authentic sexual behavior is honest and respectful. Valuing your partner's well-being demonstrates integrity and utmost love. Devote thought and planning to safeguard yourself and your partner from illness and unintended pregnancy. You create intimacy with your sexual partner with calm conversations about sensitive subjects like methods of sexual protection. Today, condoms are thinner, more sensitive, and less prone to breakage. Creating intimate bonds happen at some of the most unexpected times. Communicate!

Toys are tools. Don't expect a vibrator and other pleasure toys to do all the work. Vibrators come in many shapes, lengths, and materials. Some are water-resistant. As a starter, I suggest a battery-powered cylinder-like vibrator, the "bullet" or "pearl" or the "pocket rocket." They are easy to use with male or female partners, easy to clean and very safe. Use ample high-quality water-based lubricant to avoid vibration causing a friction-burn. Investigate some interesting pleasure toys and games, study new techniques, and adhere to proper hygiene behaviors.

During sexual arousal, all your senses are ignited. Your sensitivity to all stimulation is magnified. One particular sensation often ignored is temperature. Temperature play, in various forms, is highly erotic. A cool evening breeze from a slightly open window contrasts with the heat produced between two warm bodies during steamy sex. The heat of a warm beverage shared mouth-to-mouth toasts up a couple coming in from the cold. A steamy shower before hopping into the sheets or a slightly cool shower after overheating yourselves in passionate play invigorates your connection to your partner.

Conversation between partners galvanizes connection. Words spoken at the right time and in the right tone, along with bona fide moans and soft shrieks of ecstasy send both partners into orbital bliss. It is exciting and helpful to signal your partner; verbally or otherwise, that you are sexually soaring, especially when you are about to orgasm.

After all, you and your partner want to be good lovers. Verbal feedback confirms when you are succeeding. Genuine expression and authentic release of emotion is very powerful. Faking or falsely exaggerating audible emotion is easily detected and kills the moment. Real release releases real sounds of pleasure.

Authentically making love has phases to each session. Passionate intercourse mirrors great theatre productions or movies in that it has an opening that sets the stage and tone, some action and a closing scene. Each phase varies in length, from a few seconds to even hours, with several encores. During the closing scene, focus your awareness on the crescendo and climax while you allow the story to unfold uninhibited. While the orgasmic climax happens rather definitively, the warm afterglow and tingling sensations linger. Take the time it takes to soothe your overworked nerve endings, acknowledge and release your lover with appreciation. Again, this can take a few seconds or a few hours.

"Quickies" count! Dare to take a "quickie" almost any place, almost any time. Snag a few minutes or protect a few hours or a full weekend for different types of intimate encounters. Again, mix it up! Intimate encounters may include a tennis match, cooking session, bicycle ride, concert, reading a good book together, and writing lyrics for a song, whatever the two of you mutually enjoy!

I read a recent business news report that lingerie as a business is proving to be remarkably resilient during the current economic downturn. If fact, the more risqué the lingerie product line, the better the volume. Exotic lingerie brand, Agent Provocateur, based in Great Britain, is demonstrating strong growth heading into 2009. Garry

Hogarth, the company's CEO, claims that couples are staying at home more to save money, but still require some entertainment. He says that women are spending more money on adventurous apparel to add spice to their relationships and spark their own need to feel good about themselves. Mr. Hogarth plans to open five to ten more stores abroad this year. Agent Provocateur broke all their previous sales records for Valentine's Day in 2009.

It appears that sexual authenticity has its place in the recovery of the current global economic crisis.

Respectful and Responsible Choices

While conducting research for this chapter, I was amazed and alarmed by the lack of "sexual literacy" in contemporary society. Social norms teach you to distrust the notion of pleasure for its own sake. Pleasure is viewed in some circles as impulsive or corruptive, leading to social, emotional, and physical degradation. My research revealed some people perceive "pleasure" as sinful, reckless, irresponsible, wasteful, and lazy. I agree with the claim that pursuing sexual pleasure can be done to damaging extremes. Much as any obsessive behavior driven to the extreme carries potential risk.

Before I close this important chapter on sexual authenticity, I must express my reverence for the intense power of erotic energy. In today's society, risk-free sex does not exist. In this context, I am not just talking about pregnancy. I am talking about all sexually transferable diseases, hepatitis, herpes, HIV, and HPV. All of us in adult society have adequate information and understanding to protect ourselves from physical diseases if we make wise choices.

In my pharmacology training I came to understand how high levels of risk to human safety set the standard for proper drug administration practices. Safety is the code. Following these guidelines saves lives. We were taught five absolute maxims when administering any medication. They are:

1. Right drug
2. Right person
3. Right time

4. Right dose

5. Right method

Likewise, there are behavioral risks that I encourage you to consider as you ignite your sexual sparks. Risks are emotional, personal, and interpersonal. Respect for your partner and yourself is the code. Author, Jay Wiseman, *Tricks to Please a Woman* and *Tricks to Please a Man,* offers the following cautions. Be sexual with the:

1. Right person

2. Right way

3. Right time

4. Right location

5. Right reasons

Wiseman writes, "If any of the above are not right, then problems – sometimes very serious, severe or even life-destroying problems can emerge."

Adopt Wiseman's advice and then go out and have **FUN!** Relax, open yourself up, give and receive pleasure. Sexual authenticity is about real pleasure, connection, and intimacy.

Moments to Capture from Chapter Seven

The world could use a little more "play." Play balances life's complexity.

- Research shows pleasure, including sexual pleasure, eases stress, calms nerves and balances emotional energy.

- Sexual authenticity is your ability to experience *who-you-really-are* most fully and the ability to transfer that sensually radiant energy to your lover, receiving your lover's full authentic expression in return.

- Sexual authenticity is not goal directed.

- If you have been in your relationship for a while and feel you have lost some mystery and passion, rediscover your lover through intentionally engaging all your senses.

- Create your personal sexual journey and fill your own unique tool chest.

- Be respectful and make responsible choices. In today's society, risk-free sex does not exist. There are both physical and emotional considerations.

CHAPTER EIGHT

Professionally Authentic and Sensual

Trusting That You Are the Enterprise

What you do in work is what you do in love. What you do in love is what you are in life. Thus, your work, your love and your life all define you!

Passion and authentic sensuality integrate well in all professions. Enthusiasm, fervor, and zeal are the tool of all successful entrepreneurs. A crazed chef tantalizes your taste buds. A fastidious dentist makes your smile dazzle. An obsessed scientist discovers a cure. A determined accountant finds a hidden tax deduction.

Are you pursuing your profession with vigor because it "feels" good? Do you feel personally rewarded and pass around the good vibrations to others?

Everything you do in life has meaning. When you observe each moment, there is a purpose. The moments of your life invested in work are as important as every other moment of your life. If you spend the majority of your life working in one capacity or another, consider the tremendous importance of this time spent.

There are at least four professional pursuits worthy of your time investment.

- Professionally pursuing your heart's desire;
- Living a passionate life that integrates your profession as an important pleasurable aspect;
- Satisfying your need to provide well for your family, while allowing you to enjoy passions aside from your gainful employment;
- Taking pleasure in the atmosphere, relationships, and sense of community that your profession provides.

Create a sense of pleasure in your work, whether you are able to pursue your life's passion or if your primary work objective is to earn money to provide for your family and enjoy your time off. Be clear about why you are working and what ultimate pleasure you are pursuing. All of these pleasures reward your professional pursuits. Does your career fit into any of these categories or do you have an additional passionate pursuit you are fulfilling?

Pursuing Your Heart's Desire

Do you have a true heart's desire? Are you one of those people pursuing your heart's desire as you line your wallet? Is it possible for you to make a living pursuing your fondest dream?

I was invited to speak at a women's global leadership forum in Oslo, Norway during the fall of 2007. I was asked to prepare a presentation guiding the attendees through a process of designing their career paths with both courage and grace. I found the topic a bit challenging and open-ended. I wondered if some of the meaning in their directive to me was "lost in translation" from Norwegian to

English. I prepared my presentation and headed to the North Country, still a little confused by my assigned topic for my presentation.

However, when I arrived in Oslo and had breakfast with the keynote speaker of the event, world-recognized adventurer, Liv Arneson, I understood exactly how an individual pursues his or her career with courage and grace.

Liv and her partner in an expedition, Ann Bancroft, made history, becoming the first women to cross the entire landmass of Antarctica on foot. Notably, the men completing similar treks on foot took a narrower pathway, never crossing the widest span of Antarctica, making Liv and Ann's accomplishment even more monumental. They spent three years planning, training, and raising funds for the journey.

The journey was more than 1,700 miles, a trek lasting 94 days. Sunshine existed only a few hours a day at the end of the short Antarctic summer, they towed 250 pound sleds each, and packed a .44 magnum revolver to guard against polar bears. Temperature routinely dropped below -75 degrees Fahrenheit. Many nights, the ice under their tent creaked and shifted with the currents of the ocean beneath it.

Without a doubt, it takes enormous courage to face such extreme outdoor conditions and torturous physical challenges of Antarctica. Even with modern technology and equipment, the threat of death is very real.

During the trek, thin ice gave way beneath Liv's feet. She plunged through the surface into an endless crevasse; the bottom hidden from view, falling away into darkness. Aided by razor sharp reflexes and sheer luck, Liv clung to the rim, her supply sled nearly following her over the edge into the black hole, dragging her down with it. Ann had torn her right shoulder muscle in a separate accident. Each woman had lost more than 20 pounds from their perfectly fit bodies over the duration of the trek consisting of muscle mass and much needed body fat that neither of these women could afford to lose in tough freezing conditions.

You can image how these circumstances might bring the worst out of some people. Yet, isolated in the frozen polar landscape, Liv and Ann were never alone or hidden from public view. Three million school children across the globe followed their progress on an Internet site through a webcam as part of an educational partnership.

The educational partnership connected students to the events of the trek in real time, as well as connected the students globally to each other. Students observed the pain and the triumphs along with Liv and Ann for part of each day during the trek. Nothing was staged or edited out.

On the contrary, the story of courage did not come from crossing the Antarctic landmass. The toughest test of the trek was mustering the courage to surrender. Liv and Ann set out to cross the entire continent of Antarctica. The continent includes Ross Ice Shelf, extending another 400 miles into Southern Ocean, claimed by New Zealand. With time and the changing season working against them, the women found themselves in disastrous blizzard conditions. They faced almost constant whiteouts and days of 24-hour darkness had narrowed in on them.

To stop at the edge of the ice shelf meant failure to complete their goal. Moving forward risked not only their lives, but put the lives of rescuers in peril, in the event of an emergency.

The adventurers, Liv and Ann, set the record for crossing the largest Antarctic land mass, spanning the broadest portion of the continent, but did not cross the Ross Ice Shelf, as originally intended. The Ross Ice Shelf (a floating sheet of ice attached to the Antarctic edge extends 400 miles out into the surrounding ocean) has never been previously crossed by male or female on foot/skis).

Via satellite phone to a classroom in Minnesota, Ann expressed her appreciation and devotion to the three million school children who had shared their journey through the team's website. Ann announced their decision to abandon the trek saying, "The trip didn't belong to us alone." A young boy's voice at the other end of the satellite phone exclaimed, "You have changed my life!"

Liv and Ann made a tremendously difficult decision. They made a responsible choice for the kids and the community they had created. Many high-risk adventurers have put their own ambitions first and perished as a result. Adventurers such as these were powerfully fit and mentally brave. But true courageousness is not selfish. The mission of the expedition was not individual glory. At the moment of truth, when Liv and Ann faced the test of integrity, they showed true courage and grace.

If you are professionally pursuing your heart's desire, go forth with courage and grace.

Seamless Pursuit of Work Life Balance

The Australian freelance creative director, Claire Lloyd, is an evangelist of sensual living. "Our senses inform our whole being. They give us enjoyment and pleasure, peace and tranquility, excitement and delight. There is no better place to indulge our senses than in our own home."

My Italian-American husband, Rick and I have a home in the heart of the California wine country, in Sonoma County. For us, this location is truly heaven on Earth! You would probably agree with us, unless of course, you live in Napa County, the flip side of the same coin. But, on both sides of the mountain that divides Napa from Sonoma, we agree, wine country living embodies the essence of authentic sensual living.

The legendary vintner, Robert Mondavi said, "Wine to me is passion. It is family and friends. It's warmth of heart and generosity of spirit. Wine is culture. It's the essence of civilization and the art of living"

The process of growing wine grapes is called "viticulture." Growing grapes is an ancient art. However, now in the wine country of California and every other region around the globe that produces wine, producers perform a complex combination of science and art. Chemistry and botanical genetics have become essential practice in the wine industry. Tradition and other special knowledge and skills necessary to produce the final product – beautiful bottled wine – make wine production a lifestyle as well as a profession.

In order to make fine wine a host of factors are considered when growing wine grapes. The territory, climate and soil conditions determine the variety to be grown. Some grapes grow better in some regions than in others. Consequently, the environment in which the vines grow characterizes the flavor of the wine grape.

It is so symbolic, don't you think? The wine country atmosphere; the beauty of lush hillsides laced with delicate rows of grapevines. Temperate weather; warm sunny days and nights cooled by the ocean fog as it rolls in most summer evenings infuses the grapes and the people living in the region with a unique sweetness that is intoxicating. Can you feel the love I have for this area and the sensual way of life?!

My husband, Rick, loves to cook Italian-style food. It is artistic and nostalgic for him. Food Network's celebrity chef, Giada de Laurentiis, author of *Everyday Italian, 125 Simple and Delicious Recipes*, is his favorite role model for cooking and exemplifies his kitchen creed: "You are what you eat!"

Giada shares my husband's Italian heritage and national pride. Italian families and their friends share life in the kitchen. Relationships stay close and people take time to be with one another. Many rituals and recipes are handed down through generations. Giada professes, "We define ourselves by the food we eat and the stories we tell, as we pass plates and bowls around the table."

Both Giada and my husband think cooking is all about passion! It's about taste, smell, and touch. It's about tradition and a lot of love. Connecting with where you come from enriches your understanding of who you really are.

Giada carries on a family tradition in cooking. Her great-grandparents owned a pasta factory in Naples, Italy. Her grandfather, "nonno" in Italian, is Dino De Laurentiis, now famous as one of Hollywood's most prolific film producers, sold pasta door to door, as a young boy growing up in Naples.

After he made his fortune in the movie business, producing more than 150 films, De Laurentiis indulged his first love by opening two Italian restaurants, one in New York and one in Beverly Hills.

Giada literally grew up in the Beverly Hills restaurant, smelling the food, observing the chefs, touching everything, and sneaking tastes behind the chef's back whenever she could.

Food became part of her soul. Following college, Giada caught a plane for Paris and enrolled in a culinary school, attending school six days a week, leaving one day to explore French markets and the culture.

Upon graduation in Paris, Giada returned to California and cooked in several of the finest restaurants. One opportunity led to another and she landed her television contract with Food Network. Giada says, "I've been lucky enough to spend my life indulging my passion for food, and now I get to share my enthusiasm on my television show, with all of you, my new extended family."

The secret to her overwhelming appeal on television is not the ingredients baked into the Italian recipes Giada cooks. Moreover, it is the lifestyle she exudes before the cameras. Mario Batali, a superstar chef in his own right said, "The first thing I noticed seeing Giada's show, *Everyday Italian*, on television was that everything on the screen was beautiful—the host, the food, the scene (sometimes filmed in her own home); everything looks delicious and real and natural."

Intertwining your career into the fabric of your life can be particularly rewarding and is a fantastic way to create an authentic lifestyle that sparks your senses as well as contributes the necessary income to your bank account.

Work Hard For the Money

In your current career, are you working hard for the money, prestige, or power? These are all noble pursuits when you are professionally authentic and sensitive. Remaining authentic and sensitive as you gain professional prestige, power, and wealth requires you to be keenly self-aware, grounded in all your senses, and open to continual feedback.

Trained as a scientific researcher, I love to observe and analyze. Intriguing opportunities have been mine when I've stood alongside my husband as he participated in very high-level business and social engagements; the World Economic Forum, CEO Summits, and many other distinguished events.

I have enjoyed watching and listening to top business executives, political leaders, and even royalty engage with each other around the world, in interesting settings. I feel privileged and grateful to have these exceptional experiences.

Recent times have been increasingly challenging for those in leadership roles. Some business and political leaders have been required to make extremely tough decisions. Current leaders conduct layoffs, undergo restructuring, implement severe cost reductions, and must adopt new, often-unproven approaches to business.

Authentic leaders lead with a firm hand and a compassionate heart. Authentic leaders have respect for others and operate honestly. Honesty to an authentic leader means a higher standard than just adhering to laws and regulations. They play to win, while at the same time, they care how they win.

It is actually easy to recognize authentic leaders: They are acutely self aware, build value for their companies and for society within their professional roles. These leaders have a vision of the future, accept and understand the emerging "new world order" and are responsive to future global demands.

There are others whom I observe that miss the target. Leaders accustomed only to operating on the positive side of economic gravity, taking advantage of artificially inflated conditions. Some struggle with current socio-economic state of affairs. False structures are exposed. Heartless demonstrations of personal greed come to light.

Once you embark on a journey of authentic self-discovery, non-authentic behavior stands out like fluorescent paint under a black light. As you open yourself to living more authentically, it is likely that you too will see justice in a broader light.

A noble pursuit of power and prestige is never boastful and self-serving. Without keen self-awareness and the ability to sense your surroundings, even the most powerful can be out-performed by those in lesser positions.

The Art of War, by the Chinese military strategist Sun Tzu, has long been praised as the definitive work on military strategies and tactics and is considered the most successful book on military strategy in history. Even today, the strategies found in Sun Tzu's memoirs are applied in contemporary business management.

However, legend has it that Sun Tzu was being acknowledged for a series of brilliant victories when he boasted that he could transform anyone into a master warrior. Intrigued with a thought, the Emperor asked, "Anyone? Even my beautiful concubines?" Sun Tzu took on the challenge of organizing the Emperor's twelve concubines into a small battalion. He lined the concubines up in the royal courtyard and began instructing them in basic marching and responding to commands. The concubines scattered, finding his orders ludicrous. They collapsed into giggles and Sun Tzu was powerless.

Sun Tzu had never been defeated in battle. He was humiliated before the Emperor and admitted his failure. Sun Tzu claimed the concubines were too stupid to become warriors. The Emperor recognized that they had skillfully handed Sun Tzu his first and only defeat.

Wealth, prestige, and power come with privileges. One of the most important privileges associated with generating wealth is your right to choose where and how you invest in humanity. All contributions matter, big or small. The key principle is that you determine a way to give that is meaningful to you.

I am continually inspired by people's generosity and global vision when it comes to investing for social good. People have amazing originality when it comes to marrying their passion for life and their interest in social investment.

There are countless true stories about people improving the world with their goodwill. The one I choose to tell you now is one that is close to my heart since my husband Rick serves on the Board of Trustees for this group.

All of you know that Garth Brooks is an extraordinary musician and entertainer. What many of you may not know is that he is a passionate baseball enthusiast and obtained the opportunity to "try out" for the majors and play with the big boys a few years ago.

Garth describes it as an opportunity of a lifetime for him! He went out with all his heart into the game. He was pretty good, but the other players convinced him that he should keep his "day job" as a musician and performing superstar and leave baseball to them. Garth had a different idea. He and some buddies started the Garth Brooks Teammates for Kids Foundation. Garth tells it this way:

"We started 10 years ago with the generous help of 67 baseball players. These guys, and those who followed, understand that their efforts can make their game count for children. Today, I am very proud to be a Teammate with more than 2,200 professional athletes who have stepped-up to help the kids. These athletes, combined with our corporate partners, other Foundations, and some very special individuals have helped us generate and distribute more than $75 million dollars in cash, gifts-in-kind and scholarships."

In addition to professional baseball players, professional athletes from football, hockey, soccer, and now basketball have joined Garth's team, giving many players a mechanism to turn their sports success into philanthropy. Garth continues to lead with authenticity as he matches and magnifies other's contributions with his own talents and resources. Garth found out that a few of these athletes actually sing and play musical instruments, too! (I wonder, do you think he told them to keep their day jobs?!)

Authentic and sensitive professional character matters, especially in positions of power and leadership.

Empowering Yourself Through Your Profession

During World War II, lipstick and other women's cosmetics became very important to the US economy. How strange was it for this particular segment of consumer goods to increase production and sales when so many husbands and boyfriends were overseas fulfilling military assignments? Who were the women looking "pretty" for? For themselves, of course!

Women had joined the workforce. Women now had an income that they controlled. The cost of cosmetics was insignificant, after providing the required necessities for themselves and their families.

Lipstick made women feel good! Feeling good, in a time of emotional stress, at a manageable cost, brought increased pleasure for many women.

Feeling good involves multiple senses, applying lipstick feels nurturing, the texture is smooth, warm color enhances your natural palette and is pleasing to look at, the taste and smell are stimulating, the movement of your mouth during speech is more attractive.

Self-esteem improved for many women across the US during this period. Women's entry into the workforce expanded their identity of themselves and they felt empowered to enhance their lives in minimal ways, increasing their own pleasure in living.

Enriching Lives Through Your Profession

By now you are familiar with my love affair with the Sonoma/Napa wine country of California. One of the most influential voices in the region is Ziggy "The Wine Gal" Eschliman. Ziggy is a bit of a "muse;" she makes people's wine wishes come true. She is recognized across America and around the globe as a leading libation expert. Ziggy is highly knowledgeable and richly engaging.

Ziggy began her career as a financial advisor; yet always had a personal passion for wine. Her first foray into the business of wine came in the mid-1980s, when she became a private wine consultant to business executives. Equipped with a keen sense for business operations, she later became a partner in Tantalus Winery in Sonoma Valley.

She rapidly began driving all phases of the business, from vineyard and harvest management, sales and marketing, distribution, and customer education.

Ziggy's desire to broadly share her passion for wine led to media opportunities in radio and television. She now hosts two radio shows, the daily "On Tour" which promotes wine country events and travel, and weekly "Wine Wednesday" an extended broadcast that includes wine industry scoop, reviews, travel, and a "Wine of the Week." These shows broadcast "live" and also stream on the Internet. Ziggy performed as a guest on ABC Television's, *View From the Bay*. She appeared in *Gourmet Magazine*, *More Magazine*, and is quoted in numerous lifestyle publications. She serves as a frequent wine judge and is a dynamic guest speaker and panelist.

Ziggy acts as a powerful "voice" for some of the most successful winemakers, and at the same time, she speaks for those in the wine industry who have little or no voice at all, namely the Spanish-speaking field and winery workers. One of Ziggy's radio shows airs in Spanish, furnishing all those in the wine industry, at every level, up-to-date industry buzz.

Ziggy's professional success is magnified by her ability to develop trusting relationships and to knit people and opportunities together. She interlaces her connections in the wine industry and all other associated industries with the community at large. Her bubbling enthusiasm and enjoyment for wine is contagious!

As a driving force behind a national movement toward making wine hip, fun and accessible, Ziggy puts it plainly, "Wine has been around for centuries; the mystery is so over. It's time to get past the stuffiness and clichés. If you are not having fun, you are not on the right track." Ziggy wants people to feel as comfortable with their wine as they feel being around her.

Recently, Ziggy added a new credit to her list of accolades: Rock Star Sommelier and personal sommelier for the legendary band, JOURNEY. "Rock-n-roll and wine strike a natural chord and musicians create harmony for wine enthusiasts everywhere," claims Ziggy.

JOURNEY band member, Jonathan Cain attended one of Ziggy's famous wine dinners. Seated next to Ziggy, Jonathan asked many inquisitive wine questions. Delighted with Ziggy's wisdom and warmth, Jonathan invited Ziggy to join the band's upcoming tour as their "private wine gal." Now that's an offer that no one could refuse!

Weaving relationships is one of Ziggy's greatest skills. She introduced Jonathan to others in the wine industry. Jonathan is now joining forces with a couple of leading winemakers to produce an elite private label wine, solely for the purpose of generating income for charitable giving.

While on tour with JOURNEY, Ziggy poured wines after each performance. Each wine selection was something special. As Ziggy put it, "Rock stars are just like any one of the rest of us, they just want to relax and enjoy a really nice glass of wine after a hard day's work."

Ziggy felt the rigor of touring with a rock-n-roll band. Everywhere you go, every concert you play, everybody wants "a piece of you" if you are a rock star. You want to give all that you can to your fans. She watched the band "charge up" for events. They gave all that they had on stage. Her special gift of wine afterwards was always surprising; gave band members a little lift, something "fun" to look forward to, something exclusive just for them.

Passing benefits forward is Ziggy's way of doing good business. Her eyes and heart are wide-open, seeing opportunities in everyday life and integrating them into her way of living and giving. Ziggy enjoys volunteering for the YWCA and found an opportunity to multiply her personal contribution to the organization. As a leading wine authority, she applied her insight and local celebrity draw to attract an overcapacity crowd to a wine luncheon to benefit the Sonoma County YMCA. The event yielded record breaking returns for the YMCA and fun was had by all.

Ziggy understands life balance, having the ability to draw boundaries in order to replenish her supply of energy and zest. She lives a rich and rewarding life by creating pleasure around her. She makes life better by adding good wine, good food, and good friends. When you are around Ziggy, life is a party and everyone is invited!

You Are Never Alone in Your Success

General Colin Powell, career soldier and former US secretary of state is a fellow speaker with my husband, Rick, for a leadership seminar group called, *Get Motivated!* Listening to General Powell is always inspiring. He emphasizes that a leader never has all the insight and skills to win a conquest. A leader must be accurately self-aware and make sure he surrounds himself with people to fill all roles:

"In every successful military organization, and I suspect in all successful enterprises, different styles of leadership have to be present. If the top man has his vision, he requires a "whip hand" to enforce his ideas. If the organization has a visionary and a whip hand, it needs a "chaplain" to soften the relentless demands of the others."

My sister, Sheila, has served in the military in some capacity her entire career. Sheila began as a US Air Force medical officer, a captain, right out of graduate school. Sheila serves in medical air evacuation and other medically related roles. Over the past several years, she has completed several active duty assignments in Afghanistan and Iraq.

Last summer, we participated in Sheila's "pinning" ceremony when she became a colonel. It was a deep, emotionally moving ceremony. Sheila was presented by a private color guard and a fellow officer in full uniform sang the national anthem. The lyrics rang clear from the most beautiful tenor voice I have heard outside an opera house.

Shelia reports to a high ranking Air Force general, a powerful leader, at least six and a half feet tall, an African-American officer. When he rose to speak the room became a sanctuary. He gave such a sincere and emotionally charged tribute to my younger sister that not one of us in the room was dry-eyed.

Struck by the trust and loyalty displayed in the room, I felt envious of the comradeship and connection those who serve together feel. That day, I deeply understood how soldiers risk their lives for each other to gain victory with their co-patriots. What if all of our work teams shared that type of support and confidence in each other? How different would your attitude be toward your work?

Beauty in a Business Where You Least Expect It

Almost everyone has heard of the Pirelli annual calendar. Pirelli, an Italian automobile tire company, publishes it. Pirelli is known for its style and sensuality. But of course you say, passionate Italians with their love of beauty and the female form would dream up this flamboyant confection. Wrong! It was a British chap named Derek Forsyth, in 1962, who was in charge of advertising at the Pirelli UK subsidiary and seeking to boost his sales against the competitors, Dunlop and Goodyear.

In those days, small independent tire dealers sold mostly replacement tires. Forsyth considered his customer base, mostly hardworking family men. They would appreciate gazing at a lovely feminine silhouette alongside a beautiful vehicle clad in Pirelli products. The whole thing looked painfully contrived, but it resonated strongly with its target audience.

Now, some forty-seven years later, the Pirelli calendar thrives. For an annual outlay of two million dollars, the calendar brings in publicity worth nearly three hundred fifty million dollars each year. That's a lot of customers feeling good and buying tires!

Feel for Business

Electronic delivered news, served up instantly via the Internet and mobile devices has buried daily newspapers without even a memorial service. The demise of the daily newspaper occurred so quickly that not all the publishers have dealt properly with the deceased.

Likewise, I am unwilling to give up my beloved tactile ritual of unfolding and diving into a well-written newspaper. The experience only happens "in-print." My favorite newspaper is the *Financial Times*. It is the crown jewel of daily news publications in hardcopy.

Maybe it is the salmon colored paper it is printed on. The size is the paper is slightly smaller than many newspapers and has a little different feel to hold. Maybe it is because it is not available on every street corner. Scarcity elevates the value. Whatever the reason, I love the *Financial Times!*

The weekend edition is especially delicious. The *Life & Art* section pulses with articles that spark your senses. Pages are sprinkled with documentary-like pieces about food and drink, music and conversation, travel and human consciousness. The words and images are heartbreaking and humorous, optimistic and disturbing, hopeful and crushing. Contrasting views printed side-by-side is real life!

You can read *Financial Times* on electronic devices; my husband reads it daily on his Amazon Kindle. But I hope to hold on to my paper copy for as long as possible. I like the way it feels!

Moments to Capture from Chapter Eight

What you do in work is what you do in love. What you do in love is what you are in life. Thus, your work, your love and your life all define you!

- Passion and authentic sensuality integrate well in all professions.

- Create a sense of pleasure in your work, whether you are able to pursue your life's passion or if your primary objective is working for the money to provide for your family and enjoy your time off.

- There are at least four professional passions worthy of your time investment.

- Professionally pursuing your heart's desire;

- Living a passionate life that integrates your profession as an important pleasurable aspect;

- Satisfying your need to provide well for your family, while allowing you to enjoy passions aside from your gainful employment;

- Taking pleasure in the atmosphere, relationships and sense of community your profession provides.

CHAPTER NINE

Designing a Sensual Living Plan

The Life You Ordered Has Arrived

I wrote this book to offer you a blueprint for constructing your own authentic and sensual lifestyle. A life that is unique. A life that is satisfying. I want you to live everyday of your life, moment to moment, by your own design. This section of the book enables you to feel your way through the complexities of your life and chart a path to the rich life you deserve.

Nothing in this book was given to me by "divine revelation" or is new information. My goal was to sift through a lot of available information, examine a number of established tools, share some interesting examples in storytelling fashion, and then present a set of principles in an open format for you to assemble into a model that works for you.

Gandhi rendered many words of wisdom and one of his most quoted musings is, *"Be the change you want to see."* He uttered these words as a challenge to a nation. In this case, the test is directed only to you. It is the only pathway or option you have. You, and only you, are the author of your life's plan. You are the monarch, the strategist, the artist, and the jester in your realm of existence.

Designing a *sensual living plan* can be summed up in four simple, yet extremely important steps. It is straightforward. All you have to do to implement your plan is **FEEL**:

F – Focus on reality

E – Explore who you really are

E – Experiment with being in command of your own perspective

L – Let go of your thoughts; allow your authentic feelings to guide your behavior

Focus on reality

Focus on reality. Reality is in the moment. The past is now beyond your control. The future is out of your grasp. Living in the moment is "being-expecting" in a state of potential, and keenly aware. You observe your surroundings, knowing that there is always a pending opportunity for something very important to happen. You have the ability to decide when it is the right moment to act.

We live in a high-rise building in San Francisco. The great thing about living in a high-rise building in an urban setting is the human energy that is constantly around you, particularly the restaurants and shops in the ground floor of your building. In our building, Paragon Restaurant is on the northwest corner on the street level.

Paragon feeds us dinner most nights when we are in San Francisco (breakfast is always at South Beach Café during weekdays on the northeast corner). Above the bar at Paragon, there is an enormous mirror, extending the entire length of the bar; rising all the way to the ceiling. From anywhere is the restaurant you can see yourself in the mirror, because it reflects the entire seating area of the restaurant. When I look in that mirror, I feel the experience of looking at myself, fully in the present. I see all the other guests eating at the restaurant.

I see all the action at the bar. I see the engagement of the restaurant employees in their roles as bartender, server, chef, and manager, making their livelihoods serving us, the customers.

Look at your life as if you were looking into a mirror. Detach enough to see the big picture of what is going on. Connect with your role within the context of the big picture. Are you engaging with the "scene" in a way that meets your overall desires?

Do you see that reframing your perspective allows you to come from a bigger place? Has reality become clearer to you? Do you see that your thoughts are not reality? They are only thoughts. You assign value to your thoughts and fears. When you broaden your perspective to include the bigger scene, your thoughts and fears seem marginal. That is what I mean by allowing yourself to come from a bigger place.

Exercise

Stay in Your Body

In order to stay fully present, moment to moment, stay in your body. I mean focus on the physical you. Notice how your body is reacting to any given situation. What do you see? What do you hear? What do you feel?

Are you sweating or does your body feel cool? Are your muscles tense or relaxed? Do you feel lightheaded or clear minded? Are you alert or sleepy and dull? Do you feel pain anywhere in your body or is your body energetically alive?

These contrasting body responses are neither right nor wrong, physical responses all serve valuable purposes at their proper times. Your body is an enormous sensor, collecting data from your environment, triggering an emotional response, sending feelings to your mind to process, and then instructing your body to act. Be aware of this process. Enjoy the process. You are an extraordinary automated being, taking in data, processing it and determining an output in the form of a human reaction.

- Feel your body
- Remember that a thought is only a thought, not reality
- See the scene from a bigger place
- Be aware of the emotional messages you send your brain
- Actively, by choice, participate in your physical response

Focus Tools

Talisman

A Talisman is a symbolic object that represents a precept with a specific meaning. Select on object, such as a simple ring or bracelet that serves are a reminder to be fully present, moment-to-moment. I have read that a "sticky dot", purchased at an office supply store and placed on your steering wheel of your car can be an effective Talisman for staying focused in the present and connected with your body while driving. Change the object at the first of each month so that the reminder remains fresh. Each time you see the Talisman, check in with yourself, make sure you are "in your body" and that you are participating in life keenly aware and fully present.

Creed

A creed is an affirmation statement that you repeat aloud once a day, at the same time of day, for 30 days. Here is a statement:

There will never be another now—I'll make the most of today
There will never be another me—I'll make the most of myself

Breathing

First of all, notice your breathing. Place your hand on your abdomen and watch your hand move. Allow your abdomen to lift your hand during your inhalation as your abdomen expands and watch your hand lower as your abdomen contracts during exhalation. If the process is reversed for you, and your hand sinks into your abdomen when you inhale then your lungs are not filling fully with air. Think about your lungs expanding downward, pushing your diaphragm lower, and causing your abdomen to extend. When you exhale, allow your diaphragm to rise, sucking your abdomen inward. This is the way an infant breathes; it is the most effective way to breathe. When you are overly excited or frightened, you breathe rapidly only in your chest. It is an ineffective way to breathe. When you breathe effectively, your mind and body are balanced. Balance your breathing and you soothe your mind and your body.

Physical Exercise

Moving your body grounds you like no other activity. If you feel emotional or mental fatigue, take a walk or jog. If you are tense, stretch your muscles. If you are nervous or angry, defuse energy through physical work or repetitive power building sports. Exercise moderately and vary your routine by mixing some aerobic activities, with weights or resistance workouts, and stretching or yoga. Hike, play tennis, swim and dance. Mix it up. Being active refreshes you physically and emotionally.

Relax

Begin scanning your body, starting at your toes and slowly relaxing your feet. Feel the relaxed sensation move up your legs, muscle by muscle. Move your attention through your abdomen relaxing every muscle and organ. Feel your chest and shoulders relax. Move the focus down your arms, releasing and relaxing every muscle as you go until you have released your fingers. Allow your neck and face to relax, including your eyes and mouth. Feel your mind soften and then even your hair relax.

Multitasking

Your mind is amazing. You can actually multitask and remain fully present. But first, train yourself to be fully present while performing one task at a time. The key to multitasking is not really focusing on more than one task at once. Rapidly shift focus from one task to another for an intense split second, giving your brief full attention to each task. It can be exhilarating! When your mind blurs, return to focusing on only one task at a time. Note – people are not tasks. When communicating or engaging with another human, offer your full attention. Performing tasks together is an alternative interaction to build connection while accomplishing tasks. Authenticity means "showing up" for other people. Giving your authentic self to others in relationships anchored by mutual respect enriches your life like nothing else.

Explore

The actor, Alan Arkin, once said, "When you start discovering who and what you are, it's bigger than anything you ever imagined yourself to be. By definition, it is generous. It's a generous exploration. The more you that you find, the more of you there is to give to those you love."

As Colin Powell's quote earlier demonstrated, no one person can possess all of the best human characteristics. Having a unique subset of characteristics make you valuable to society and give you an opportunity to fine tune the very best of yourself.

Exploring who you really are can be frightening at the beginning. Approach exploration as an adventure. Tell yourself the truth. As silly as it sounds, you may be in the habit of frequently lying to yourself. Don't cheat. Undertake self-exploration with full integrity. You will like the real person you reveal. Don't expect yourself to be perfect.

Exploration – Exercises

Self-exploration is about self-acceptance. As you accept yourself, you increase your capacity to accept others and work in the world with more effectiveness. Accept that you are not perfect. Find your sense of humor, lightheartedness about your imperfections makes your strengths shine more brightly.

Discover pleasure in your authentic approach to life. Anything that feels good to your soul is taking you in the right direction. Have clear and strong intentions. You will eventually arrive at the place you have been moving toward. There are many paths to your goals if your intentions are clear.

Listen to the compliments that others give you. Feel love and gratitude coming toward you. Sense and enjoy the warmth of human kindness.

Exploration Tools

There are many tools of psychology for personal discovery. I have a personal favorite that I recommend you try. Martin E. P. Seligman, Ph.D. author of the book, *Authentic Happiness,* is a professor at the University of Pennsylvania Authentic Happiness Center, and developed my favorite technique. It is my favorite tool because all character traits revealed by the questionnaire are equally valued; it is non-competitive, no one scores above anyone else.

Dr. Seligman developed the *VIA Signature Strengths Questionnaire*, containing 240 questions rating 24 specific personal characteristics. The acronym "VIA" stands for "Values in Action." The tool identifies your five highest scoring character strengths.

Pay attention to the top five and find ways in your life to use them more often. These strengths come easily to you. They are your natural gifts. Develop your highest strengths throughout your life to improve your health, your relationships, and your career. Identifying your strongest traits empowers you to give more to the world around you and to achieve new levels of authentic satisfaction, pleasure, and meaning in your life.

You can access the questionnaire online at the University of Pennsylvania Authentic Happiness Center website. It is free of charge and is scored electronically, providing immediate results:

www.authentichappiness.sas.upenn.edu

Here is a complete list of the 24 characteristics. Characteristics are not listed in any particular order below. The electronic questionnaire will rank your characteristics according to your strengths. Be honest and answer the questions authentically. That is the only way to make the results valuable to you in your journey of self-exploration.

Appreciation of beauty and excellence   You notice and appreciate beauty, excellence, and/or skilled performance in all domains of life, from nature to art to mathematics to science to everyday experience.

Capacity to love and be loved   You value close relations with others, in particular those in which sharing and caring are reciprocated. The people to whom you feel most close are the same people who feel most close to you.

Curiosity and interest in the world   You are curious about everything. You are always asking questions, and you find all subjects and topics fascinating. You like exploration and discovery.

Gratitude   You are aware of the good things that happen to you, and you never take them for granted. Your friends and family members know that you are a grateful person because you always take the time to express your thanks.

Humor and playfulness You like to laugh and tease. Bringing smiles to other people is important to you. You try to see the light side of all situations.

Creativity, ingenuity, and originality Thinking of new ways to do things is a crucial part of who you are. You are never content with doing something the conventional way if a better way is possible.

Forgiveness and mercy You forgive those who have done you wrong. You always give people a second chance. Your guiding principle is mercy and not revenge.

Kindness and generosity You are kind and generous to others, and you are never too busy to do a favor. You enjoy doing good deeds for others, even if you do not know them well.

Leadership You excel at the tasks of leadership: encouraging a group to get things done and preserving harmony within the group by making everyone feel included. You do a good job organizing activities and seeing that they happen.

Social intelligence You are aware of the motives and feelings of other people. You know what to do to fit in to different social situations and you know what to do to put others at ease.

Zest, enthusiasm, and energy Regardless of what you do, you approach it with excitement and energy. You never do anything halfway or halfheartedly. For you, life is an adventure.

Fairness, equity, and justice Treating all people fairly is one of your abiding principles. You do not let your personal feelings bias your decisions about other people. You give everyone a chance.

Hope, optimism, and future-mindedness You expect the best in the future, and you work to achieve it. You believe that the future is something that you can control.

Bravery and valor You are a courageous person who does not shrink from threat, challenge, difficulty, or pain. You speak up for what is right even if there is opposition. You act on your convictions.

Industry, diligence, and perseverance You work hard to finish what you start. No matter the project, you "get it out the door" in timely fashion. You do not get distracted when you work, and you take satisfaction in completing tasks.

Perspective (wisdom) Although you may not think of yourself as wise, your friends hold this view of you. They value your perspective on matters and turn to you for advice. You have a way of looking at the world that makes sense to others and to yourself.

Self-control and self-regulation You self-consciously regulate what you feel and what you do. You are a disciplined person. You are in control of your appetites and your emotions, not vice versa.

Love of learning You love learning new things, whether in a class or on your own. You have always loved school, reading, and museums – for you: anywhere and everywhere there is an opportunity to learn.

Honesty, authenticity, and genuineness You are an honest person, not only by speaking the truth but by living your life in a genuine and authentic way. You are down-to-earth and without pretense; you are a "real" person.

Citizenship, teamwork, and loyalty   You excel as a member of a group. You are a loyal and dedicated teammate, you always do your share, and you work hard for the success of your team.

Spirituality, sense of purpose, and faith   You have strong and coherent beliefs about the higher purpose and meaning of the universe. You know where you fit in the larger scheme of things. Your beliefs shape your actions and are a source of comfort to you.

Judgment, critical thinking, and open-mindedness   Thinking things through and examining them from all sides are important aspects of who you are. You do not jump to conclusions, and you rely only on solid evidence to make your decisions. You are able to change your mind.

Modesty and humility   You do not seek the spotlight, preferring to let your accomplishments speak for themselves. You do not regard yourself as special, and others recognize and value your modesty.

Caution, prudence, and discretion   You are a careful person and your choices are consistently prudent ones. You do not say or do things that you might later regret.

Once you have identified a set of character traits that come naturally to you, Dr. Seligman explains in his book and on the University of Pennsylvania website how best to apply your results. He encourages you to use your new insight to enrich your personal happiness and magnify your success. Remember, the purpose of the exercise is to increase your personal awareness and reinforce your innate strengths.

Experiment

Happiness is not something you find, but rather something you create. Pleasure and reward do not always show up in your life how you might expect it. The most satisfying situations in your professional life might unfold quite unforeseen. Living a rich life means you are willing to experiment a little as you go, developing awareness, agility, and an attitude that is open to outcome.

At the end of January in 2009, Christie Hefner stepped down from her role as Chairman and CEO of Playboy Enterprises after leading the company for nearly 22 years. She grew magazine sales worldwide to exceed nine million copies monthly, launched Playboy Television and established Playboy's powerful Internet presence. Each media offering's business format is very different from the other. Television required more "action" than print. Articles and images from the magazine cannot be converted to television programming. The Internet requires an interactive real-time engagement that neither television nor print provides. Pioneering Playboy media was one of Christie's undisputed successes.

Shortly after her departure, I attended a group breakfast with Christie. I was very impressed by her warmth and authenticity. I had long admired her activism for women's rights, free speech, and freedom of the press. She caught my attention years ago when she established the Hugh M. Hefner First Amendment Awards, honoring her father in 1979. Christie had dreams of becoming a journalist or an attorney. Her employment at Playboy was initially to be only temporary. Christie had an entrepreneurial spirit and enjoyed a democratic way of conducting business at Playboy. She was comfortable with creative risk in business.

When faced with accusations of "sexism" and the exploitation of women in the company, Christie challenged accusers to find women at any level in the company that felt exploited; quite the contrary, women at Playboy overwhelmingly felt empowered. Surveys showed women at Playboy felt highly valued and received fair and equal treatment and compensation at the company. At breakfast that morning, Christie called it the Rorschach effect, in that Playboy had a mirror-like effect, reflecting people's true nature, exposing their values and discomforts.

The professional story of Christie Hefner is an example of "bold experimentation." Experimentation is never timid. Bold is not careless. Bold is not reckless. Bold is moving forward with confidence and keen awareness, ready for potential hazards or obstacles, and the agility to stay on course with flexible adjustments.

Experimentation – Exercises

Identify what symbolizes your aspirations. Study others. Reflect on others and what attributes have lead to their success. If your intention is to become a benevolent leader, who is both hardheaded and softhearted, picture a character like King Arthur of Camelot. Having a symbol clarifies your vision of what success looks like and models the necessary behaviors to achieve your goal.

Get away regularly. The best way to self-reflect is to change the scene. Changing your surroundings refreshes your senses and vitalizes your mind. A physical change of perspective often creates a space in your mind for new ways of seeing things. If you can't physically get away often enough, vary your daily routine. Habits become mindless. To refresh your mind, break your habits.

Set your own stage. Create your own living and working environment. Consider all of your senses as you design the spaces where you spend your time. Embellish your surroundings echoing your values and with esthetics that soothe your senses will ignite your passions.

Approach learning as experimentation. Learning is experienced as personal transformation. It is impossible to "gather" information and call it learning. As learning occurs, you become a different person. You are never the same. You cannot return to a point before you gained new insight. Learning is a way of being. You become a new person.

Virtual experiences expand your real world. Today, a rich real life experience incorporates the virtual world. Interfacing with others around the globe, professionally and personally expands your view. Virtual work groups and online communities provide opportunities for you to live fully present as a global citizen. Connecting with others that share your passions make the world a more cohesive place. You will find that you have more in common with others outside your realm than you might have expected. Finding solutions to almost any question you have is possible when you can connect with others beyond your current scope. Note: Absolute authenticity and integrity is the rule when engaging in virtual experiences. Remember, **truth** is what this journey is all about. It is your opportunity to be your best you in the world; including in cyber-worlds.

Experimentation – Tools

Master your ability to ignite your senses through visualization. In a quiet place, clear your mind and relax your body with the techniques taught in the section **Focus Tools** above. Pick a backdrop that is alluring to you. Picture every detail of the scene in your mind. Place yourself in your imaginary setting. Turn on your senses and experience the scene as if you were there; the sights, sounds, tastes, smells, your feelings about being there. If you need help getting started, visualize a beach, feel the sand beneath your feet, see the waves, hear the seagulls, feel the wind, taste the salt in the air, emotionally experience the scene, tell yourself a story of what is happening to you while you are on the beach. Next time design your own scene!

Express your emotions and intentions in writing. Journaling is a powerful method of organizing your intentions. Write in your diary; record your activities, feelings, and desires. Feelings expressed become dreams. Dreams become reality and your diary documents your progress and growth. I prefer writing electronically; it is faster for me. However, you may enjoy handwriting with pen and paper. Share your passions in your own blog. Contribute to the blogs of others with similar interests. Express your feelings for those you care about in writing.

Vary your routine. Mix it up. Spice it up! Drive a different pathway to your usual destination. See new surroundings. Take day trips in a car, a boat, a motorcycle, a bicycle, walking, on horseback, or in a rickshaw. All modes of transportation offer a variety of sensual experiences. Explore new neighborhoods and shops. Go to your usual haunts at different times of the day, a different season, during different types of weather. Ski resorts are fabulous during the summer; especially for biking, hiking and horseback riding. Go to the beach in bad weather. Experience the power of the ocean during a storm (from a safe spot, of course). Have breakfast at the restaurant you typically frequent for happy hour following work. It will be a completely different experience and the service staff will be completely new faces.

Rearrange your home and workspace. Discard clutter. Donate what you no longer use. Ignite your senses by changing your environment. Set the mood. Create different moods in different spaces. Intensify lighting to brighten areas and mute lighting to soften others. Add energy to your kitchen with vibrant colors. Freshen your bathrooms with pure white linens with minimal accents of color. Add candles for light effects and pleasing scents. Add a fragrance like lemon grass to your entry with scented oil and bamboo reeds. As you walk through the door, your senses will welcome you home. Integrate sound into your environment. Music or soft ambient sounds of nature or falling water complement your home with peaceful tones. Do you have a pet? Does a pet enhance or inhibit your lifestyle? Sensual living uniquely reflects you. Create a place where you can celebrate your life, alone and with others: a place to rejuvenate your soul.

Dress yourself like you mean it. What does your attire tell the world about you? Revamp your wardrobe. You do not need to buy new clothes. Accent with a scarf or tie of a different color. Wear new socks or underwear, especially if no one but you knows what you're wearing!

Participate in lifelong learning. What hobby or recreation have you always wanted to do? Learn a new sport. Play a musical instrument or start voice lessons. Dance or do martial arts. Study a new language and plan travel to use your language skills.

Use intoxicants judiciously. Light intoxication can relax you, brighten your mood, helps release your inhibitions. But, avoid clouding your judgment, dulling your senses and impairing your coordination. Sensitivity suffers and authentic pleasure is impossible when heavily intoxicated.

Let Go!

Let go of your thoughts. Allow your authentic feelings to guide you. Simply put, "Experience the experience!"

Create an authentic connection with whatever is going on in the moment. Professionally, personally, in pleasure and in pain, stay with the "feeling." Thoughts distract you, especially when you feel fear or anxiety. You try to "think your way out" of uncomfortable feelings.

Buddhist Saint, Milarepa, admonished followers to, "Maintain the state of undistractedness and distractions will fly off."

Legend tells of Milarepa living in a cave. He was visited by demons of the lower path (Hinayana). The demons demanded entry.

Milarepa refused them entry, argued with them, pleaded with them, fought with them. The demons persisted. Finally, in complete frustration, Milarepa invited the demons into his cave and offered them tea. Instantly, the demons disappeared!

Describing his realization, Milarepa explained, "I have understood this body of mine to be the product of ignorance, composed of flesh and blood and lit up by the perceptive power of consciousness. To those fortunate ones who long for emancipation it may be the great vessel by which they may procure Freedom. But to the unfortunates, it may be the guide to lower and miserable states of existence. Your life is the boundary mark whence you may take an upward or downward path. Our present time is a most precious time, wherein each of us must decide, in one way or other, for lasting good or lasting ill."

Remember the last time you felt stage fright? Do you recall the gripping sensation of fear racing through your body? Remember your heart pounding in your chest and your tight and shallow breathing? Remember the fluttering feeling in your stomach and weakness in your knees? Do you now understand that these are symptoms only of the thoughts you create, not reality?

To move through the feeling of fear—acceptance is the right response. Separate your thoughts from your feelings. Experience only feelings. Acknowledge them for what they are, authentic feelings and part of your natural physical and emotional response. Fear lessens and will eventually dissolve along with all the uncomfortable sensations.

In the future, when you feel stage fright, embrace it. Feel the feelings and get energized by it. Move the energy to your feet or whatever area of your body needs strength.

The same simple principle of letting go of the thought and allowing authentic feelings apply to pleasure. Dogen, Master of enlightenment prophesizes, "Zen is simply the easy and pleasant practice of a Buddha, the realization of the Buddha's Wisdom. To know yourself is to forget yourself."

You don't have to study 12th century proverbs to receive divine counsel. During the final editing phase of this book, my husband, Rick and I were invited to attend a breakfast in San Francisco with His

Holiness the 14th Dalai Lama. It was a small gathering and the topic of discussion was "The Joy of Giving." The breakfast was sponsored by the organization, "The Forgotten International" whose mission is to bring together people in the world who have great resources with people who have great needs in order to help alleviate poverty and suffering.

The wisdom spoken by the Dalai Lama that morning that sticks in my mind most pertains to "peace." His Holiness said, "Non-violence is more important than peace. Building guns to ensure peace is not peaceful." The conversation lasted about 90 minutes. The Dalai Lama has a hearty sense of humor that translates well into any language.

In closing, his final message was clear and simple, "If you want to feel blessed, work with all those around you who have so little and suffer so much. In doing so, you will feel blessed in return." Everyone in the room had received plain guidance directly from the ultimate authority on peace, love, and happiness, his formula for creating joy.

You have daily opportunities to follow Dalai Lama's directive. Both Rick and I travel about 200,000 air miles a year on commercial airlines. If you have flown on commercial airlines lately, you know how dramatically air travel has changed. Air travel sometimes feels like "survival of the fittest." Cancelled and overbooked flights can be frustrating to business travelers and daunting to infrequent travelers that are unfamiliar with travel systems.

Rick has made it a habit when flying to reach out and connect with travelers in need. He has carried bags down the jet way for elderly passengers, given tips to foreign visitors on how to get rebooked on cancelled flights, and given a listening ear to folks who just feel like nobody understands the disappointment they feel when they have missed the only connection to a small town where their niece is getting married later that same afternoon.

Most of the time, these are not heroic acts. These are only acts of human kindness. Giving the gift of kindness costs you nothing. Yet, giving kindness miraculously alleviates Rick's own sense of frustration, if only for a brief period of time. Reaching out to others, with the intention to serve, with no expectation of return, rewards you with a sense of power and influence over situations that appear out of your control. You are no longer a victim of an unfortunate circumstance. You feel pleasure, knowing that the world has been made a little better for someone, just because you were there.

Acts of kindness are sometimes large and sometimes small. The most important point is to "act" when your senses and your emotions prompt you. Last fall, Rick and I traveled to Ngeruka, a remote rural village located near the epicenter of the 1994 genocide in Rwanda, East Africa. We negotiated an agreement and visited the proposed site for a new health center to provide care for more than 25,000 people in the region, funded by the Garth Brook's Teammates for Kids Foundation.

When our SUV pulled into the village, swarms of barefoot and dusty children descended on us with the biggest brightest smiles you have ever seen. Running water would be a luxury in this village. Rainwater is collected for consumption and all other purposes, typically in big banana leaves.

Two weary nurses met us. These two women have the over-whelming job of providing all the current health services to Ngeruka region, treating all injuries and burns, diseases, and delivering all newborn babies who make it to the two room health post.

In this region, a single blade machete is the most essential farm tool.

Leaning against the doorway of the health post was a farmer that must have suffered a machete injury and was missing much of his left check and jaw. He held his face in a bloody cloth waiting for his turn to see one of the nurses. Rick has never been very good around blood and I instantly wanted to shield him from the scene, but it was too late. Almost immediately, Rick emotionally connected with the people of Ngeruka.

When we left the health post, he took me aside and said, "The Belluzzo family will adopt this village. We will even build soccer fields and playgrounds. A family with an Italian heritage like ours must build soccer fields (Italians love European football) and playgrounds for these beautiful children." We contacted a Canadian organization called "Right to Play" to implement our plan. Right to Play designed the ball fields and playgrounds, as well as a school program for physical fitness that integrates HIV/AIDS awareness and other health related activities into the play.

Act when the emotion moves you.

How many times have you found yourself in a perfectly pleasurable situation or a beautiful place and you slipped inside your head wondering how long something this good could possibly last or you wish you could be with a loved one to experience the same scene? If you do let your mind drift, you lose the richness of the moment.

When you exit the scene and enter your thoughts, the magnitude of the moment is lost. You can never recapture it. If you bring your loved one back to the scene, it might be wonderful, but it will not be the same scene that you experienced before. It will be a new scene, worthy of your full attention.

Now, reminisce the last time when you were so engrossed in an activity that you could think of nothing else. Time stood still. Your senses worked together in harmony, making the activity almost effortless.

I love to snow ski. When I am gliding down the frozen slope, my eyes fixed downhill, my knees bent to feel the contours of the mountain and absorb bumps in the terrain, I hear a "swoosh" as the edges of my skis carve turns in the snow, I feel the chill of cold air on my face, my body is warm and damp, and my heart beats fast from physical exertion. My body is pulsing with pleasure and nothing else in the world exists but this moment. I am skiing! Nothing more.

Let Go! - Exercises

There are 3 ways to "forget yourself" and Let Go!

Let go of your thoughts and accept your feelings. Particularly during pain, fear, or anxiety, your mind goes into overdrive. Stay in your body and observe each feeling that comes up. Attach no judgment. Only observe and experience the feeling.

Let go of your ego and reach out to others. Notice and acknowledge those around you. Be generous with your spirit. It costs you nothing to share yourself. Listen to understand. Empathize and ask questions. Alter perceptions of reality by affecting how people around you feel about what is going on, especially how they feel about harsh realities. Reach out to others at the moment your senses and emotions signal to act. Do not wait, less your thoughts will go to work at convincing you otherwise. Kindness is never a bad idea.

Let go of time and feel total concentration. Make time stand still. Immerse yourself in the present moment. Notice all of your senses engage in the present. Express yourself with emotion. Let your body flow in sync with the task at hand. Focus your concentration moment to moment, not on the end game.

Let Go! - Tools

Identify situations that typically cause you fear, anxiety, or some type of emotional discomfort that usually leads to a physical response. The first situation that comes to my mind is driving over the crest of a hill; realizing that I am driving considerably too fast and I spot a state highway police car pulling away from the curb, accelerating behind me. Do you feel the rush of adrenalin I feel? Do you have the same knot in your stomach and weakness in your knees? Are the patrol car's lights flashing? Not yet! What thoughts are racing through your mind?

- Immediately recognize your thoughts are not reality.
- Feel the physical signals your emotions have triggered; one by one.
- Stay with the physical sensations; name the feelings: my pulse has increased, I am sweating, my face warms, and my knees feel weak.
- Send excess energy of your rapid pulse to your weak knees, balancing your strength.
- Continue to notice the sensations until they begin to dissipate.
- Once the uncomfortable sensations have ceased, take in a full cleansing breath, hold for a few seconds, and then exhale slowly.
- Notice how peaceful and powerful you feel after experiencing the experience.
- Most likely the "threat" has passed. If the threat remains, you are now clear minded and have the capability to manage the peril.

Be generous of spirit. Look for opportunities to give more than you receive. Be keenly aware of people and situations around you. Be ready to act when emotions moves you. When in casual contact with others, at the market, on the roadway, at your workplace, offer respect and courtesy unconditionally. An act of kindness is never insignificant. Even a smile.

Once a day, participate in an activity so consuming that it is impossible for your mind to drift from the task at hand. It can be an all-consuming skill you have previously trained to do a new skill that requires a level of focus that you are unable to break concentration for more than a moment. Exercising your mind daily increases your ability to immerse yourself completely in a task. Soon you feel improved concentration and enjoy your ability to make time stand still.

Graduate Course: Designing Your Life

For those of you that are enjoying this book, yet feel you are already living an authentic sensual life, I challenge you to continue your quest; magnifying your personal refinement. Take your journey to the next level.

My personal coach, Lauralee Alben, gifted artist, designer, teacher, and counselor lead me through a course of personal discovery in three beautiful phases:

- Designing a Self Worth Celebrating
- Designing Work Worth Doing
- Designing a Legacy Worth Leaving

Lauralee's coaching style is experiential and hands on. She uses an ocean metaphor in her Sea Change Design Process to guide her clients on a journey of self-discovery and transformation. I learned to intentionally design the ripple effect of my life; to explore below the surface where the deep layers of myself align physically, cognitively, emotionally, and spiritually; to harness currents that produce unending cycles of energy and ideas; and to generate a flow of results that yield beauty, prosperity, creativity, well being, joy, love, and community.

I continue to pursue my true path, using my profoundly meaningful map for implementing a livelihood worth doing, a personal life worth living and an obtainable plan to achieve an enduring legacy. I completed my course with Lauralee equipped with a new way of being. It is now my responsibility to keep the torch burning and to finish the race, triumphant.

Moments to Capture from Chapter Nine

Designing a *sensual living plan* can be summed up in four simple, yet extremely important steps. It is straightforward. All you have to do to implement your plan is **FEEL**:

> **F** – Focus on reality
>
> **E** – Explore who you really are
>
> **E** – Experiment with being in command of your own perspective
>
> **L** – Let go of your thoughts; allow your authentic feelings to guide your behavior

For those of you already living an authentic sensual life, take your journey to the next level.

In the end, it is about meaning. We all want to feel our life has value. We want to know that we have truly lived, moment to moment.

Final Thoughts

With Your Boarding Pass in Hand, Your Life Soon Takes Off!

View life as a never-ending journey; accept yourself and accept making mistakes; celebrating the learning as you go. You are free to make changes when you have an outlook on life that is moment to moment. The future is always a blank page.

The most important piece of the journey is to go with people you care about and that you respect. Draw in people that give you authentic feedback and unconditional love. There is no time in life to waste on false friends and relationships that deplete your resources for less than honorable motives.

Back in chapters one and two, I left my personal story hanging. By now you know I have not walked in front of any more moving trains. But, as discussed in chapter five, human emotional framework is comprised of your inherited DNA characteristics, your circumstances and the voluntary choices you make. My journey continues to reflect all three elements of my unique emotional framework. I often feel the urge to listen to my thoughts rather than my emotional heart.

My father, a successful cattleman, bred some of the most prized livestock in the country. He approached raising children as seriously as he did breeding livestock. Growing up in school, straight "A" grades were just measuring up in my father's eyes. As children, we were bred and trained to excel.

Combine my upbringing, my baptism and marriage in the Roman Catholic Church, lifelong habits of overachieving, and an unhealthy desire to please; it is clear why carrying around a heavy dose of guilt is second nature to me.

My husband, Rick claims I am a Ferrari – not always a safe or steady ride, but incredibly fun and sexy, even when standing still. Frankly, Rick and I are both high-octane people, often running on a collision course with each other. We determined, after traveling a rather risky stretch together on a slippery road that our complex relationship is well worth taking this journey as partners. If we are skilled high performance drivers then the journey is exhilarating. As we face challenges at high speeds in the future, we hope to be prepared to handle the tight hairpin curves. Suffice it to say, Rick and I are committed and determined to support each other as pit crew for each other as well as our mutual need to be the driver behind the wheel of the car.

This book trains you to be a racecar driver, alert, with razor sharp focus. Developing this type of personal presence is not always easy. Your journey of sensual living is about taking two or three steps forward and one step back on the road to gaining greater authenticity. Habits are powerful forces. The journey does not abruptly end if you "zone out" from time to time. Each moment is new, providing a fresh opportunity to kick-start the authenticity process, if your engine stalls.

Living an authentically sensual life is far from calm. Authentic sensual living is peaceful and rich with pleasures and emotions. Do not doubt that the center of peace resides in the eye of a hurricane. Zen masters feel and experience life at its fullest, hatred and love, war and harmony, a gamut of feelings, keenly aware, fully present and yet, continually exuding peace and tranquility.

Peace occurs in turbulent times. You can only taste peace if you have been in the very heart of a battle. In the 1940s the world was at war. Here in the United States a sense of love, peace, and fierceness abounded. The American people lived with their senses ignited, aware of worldwide events and their connectedness to them, possibly more than today.

Factories and assembly lines ran night and day, candles glowed and voices sang during prayer vigils, families relinquished eggs and cheese to nourish their boys on the front lines, warm handshakes were extended to strangers and friends alike, peace raged on the home front as the troops battled a world away. There was no distance between the conflict and the hearts and minds of America.

During stillness, huge amounts of potential energy build up, ready to respond. Be ever ready to respond. Live your life surrounded by pleasing aesthetics, interesting people, and a balance of diversion.

Are you now ready to live with your senses ignited?!

AFTERWORD

Georges M. Halpern, MD, PhD
Distinguished Professor of Pharmaceutical Sciences
The Hong Kong Polytechnic University

We are what we eat...and drink. What people consume can either help or worsen their condition. Food is medicine, and many medicines were (are) foods, as we know from the Asian traditions. But the single one **major** variable that **never** appears in any medical study is the *role of pleasure.*

When did Pleasure Start?

Dr. Michel Cabanac of the Université Laval, Québec, Canada, answered this question. The sensation of touch, gentle handling of mammals (rats, mice) and lizards (Iguana), elevates the set point for body temperature, producing an emotional fever, a pleasure response. Heart rate, another detector of emotion in mammals, accelerates with gentle touch. The same is not true for frogs and fish.

These findings would suggest that emotion emerged in the evolutionary lineage between amphibians and reptiles. Such a conclusion would imply that reptiles possess consciousness with its characteristic affective dimension, pleasure. The role of sensory pleasure in decision-making was verified in iguanas placed in a motivational conflict. To be able to reach the bait (lettuce), the iguanas had to leave a warm refuge, provided with standard food, and venture into a cold environment.

The results showed that lettuce was not necessary to the iguanas and that they traded off the palatability of the bait against the disadvantage of the cold. Thus, the behavior of the iguanas was likely to be produced, as it is in humans, through the maximization of sensory pleasure. Altogether, these results may indicate that the first elements of mental experience emerged between amphibians and reptiles.

Now, to a discussion of human pleasures!

Stress vs. Pleasure

The notion that stress makes you sick and belief makes you well has been part of the popular culture for thousands of years. Stress impacts health by modulating the rate of cellular aging. There is now evidence that psychological stress – both perceived stress and chronic nature of stress, is significantly associated with higher oxidative stress, lower telomerase activity, and shorter telomere length, which are known determinants of cell senescence and longevity, in healthy premenopausal women.

The brain talks directly to the immune system, sending commands that control the body's inflammatory response to infection and autoimmune diseases. Researcher, Kevin J. Stacey has demonstrated that stimulation of the *vagus* nerve (through the release of acetylcholine) could block a rogue inflammatory response and treat a number of diseases, including life-threatening sepsis, inflammatory bowel disease, rheumatoid arthritis, type 2 diabetes, and other conditions of excessive cytokine release. It also enables consideration of the neurological basis of complementary and alternative medical therapies, such as meditation and acupuncture. He calls this network "the inflammatory reflex."

Pleasantness is the principal perceptual aspect of olfaction, your sense of smell. Pleasantness is the primary perceptual aspect humans use to discriminate odorants/fragrances or combine them into groups.

Studies with newborns suggest that at least some aspects of olfactory pleasantness may be innate. It is clearly the hedonic meaning of odor that dominates odor perception. Newborns' attraction to the scent of their mother or the sweet aroma of her milk guides infants to the breast.

The olfactory system is known for plasticity at multiple levels, which reflects an advantageous evolutionary mechanism. To automatically reject food that smells fermented is generally a safe bet.

However, if through experience one learns that exceptions exist, and for example fermented fish can be both tasty and healthy, than its pleasantness representation may shift. This is what allows Swedes to enjoy their Surströmming Herring (a dish not for the faint of heart), although even they will not say they like the odor *per se*.

The Pleasure of Food

"The pleasures of the table are for every man, of every land, and no matter of what place in history or society; they can be a part of all other pleasures and they last the longest, to console us when we have outlived the rest".
—French author, J. A. Brillat-Savarin, 1825

An increasing proportion of food consumption appears to be driven by pleasure, not just by the need for calories. The food environment may be creating an appetitive counterpart to the psychological effects of other hedonically-driven activities such as drug use and compulsive gambling. Homeostatic (i.e., eating because of physical need) and hedonic (eating for pleasure in the absence of need) eating motives overlap but are nonetheless separable. Some individuals may experience frequent thoughts, feelings and urges about food in the absence of any short-or long-term energy deficit.

Delicious food can itself create powerful motives to keep eating it, much like more traditional addictive substances. In environments where such foods are always available, such motives may continue to manifest themselves in food-related thoughts and urges even when we are away from food. The smell of freshly baked doughnuts can entice someone to stop at a bakery and eat the doughnut or the sight of a dessert can attract a person to eat even when physically full after dinner. Once such habits are firmly established, trying to change them may not be a matter of "just saying no;" rather, such discontinuation may produce withdrawal responses.

Traditionally, it has been thought that food is a form of self-medication for stress or boredom, but we should look beyond psychological factors when studying the facts behind superfluous eating. For one, rather than viewing such eating as pure indulgence, eating for pleasure may have been an evolutionary adaptation that helped us survive periods of food scarcity in the distant past.

Palatable foods may create powerful motivations to eat not only because their taste is rewarding but also because their consumption prevents the anxiety or stress that would occur if they were not consumed. Most normal-weight restrained eaters are trying to control their food intake not to lose weight but to prevent overeating and weight gain. It is logical to expect that the combination of susceptibility toward overeating and conscious efforts to avoid overeating would result in more frequent instances of "hedonic hunger."

The Pleasure of Love

Love is more than sex. Barry R. Komisaruk, PhD and Beverly Whipple, PhD, RN, both professors of physiology at Rutgers University define "love" as one's having stimulation that one desires. The nature of the stimulation can range on a continuum from the most abstract-cognitive, to the most direct-sensory, forms. Thus, this definition of love encompasses having an emotional bond with a person for whom one yearns, as well as having sensory stimulation that one desires.

They propose a neural mechanism by which deprivation of love may generate endogenous, compensatory sensory stimulation that manifests itself as psychosomatic illness. In addition, they also propose a neuroendocrine mechanism underlying sexual response and orgasm. The latter includes vaginocervical sensory pathways to the brain that can produce analgesia, release ocytocin, and/or bypass the spinal cord via the vagus nerve. They present evidence of the existence of non-genital orgasms, which suggests that genital orgasm is a special case of a more pervasive orgasmic process.

The better our understanding of love, the greater is our respect for the significance and potency of its role in mental and physical health.

The Pleasure of Music

Music is powerful. Experience the power of music, the enchantment, the visceral emotions, the tears and the joys.

A group from McGill University, in Canada, used positron emission tomography to study neural mechanisms underlying intensely pleasant emotional responses to music. Cerebral blood flow changes were measured in response to subject-selected music that elicited the highly pleasurable experience of "shivers-down-the-spine" or "chills." Subjective reports of chills were accompanied by changes in heart rate and respiration.

As intensity of these chills increased, cerebral blood flow increases and decreases were observed in brain regions thought to be involved in reward/motivation, emotion, and arousal, including ventral striatum, midbrain, amygdala, orbitofrontal cortex, and ventral medial prefrontal cortex.

These brain structures are known to be active in response to other euphoria-inducing stimuli, such as food, sex, and drugs of abuse. This finding links music with biologically relevant, survival-related stimuli via their common recruitment of brain circuitry involved in pleasure and reward.

The Pleasure of Art

I started with music, but in fact I should have with painting, and all the visual arts. My mother was a remarkable artist. At the age of 19, she was sent from Warsaw (Poland) to the *Ecole des Arts Décoratifs* in Paris. She was very talented. She mastered painting, decorative arts of lots of supports and media, ceramics, weaving and knitting, and the rest. She designed special fabrics for the high fashion like Paul Poiret, and painted theater stage sets.

We wore unique sweaters, most of the time ashamed of them since we were singled out; but we were also proud: "*Vive la Différence!*" She painted beautiful watercolors that still serve as a journal through our flights during the Second World War; and she managed to keep them!

She had known and befriended the artists who flocked to Paris between the two world wars, and, later, they came to our house: Mané Katz, Zadkine, Jean and Raoul Dufy (a patient of my father), Matisse, and many, many more whose names I have forgotten. They brought her their drawings, lithographs, paintings, sculptures. My adolescence was surrounded by art.

My mother also collected the first "coffee table" art books published in Switzerland by Albert Skira; I spent innumerable hours reading, absorbing, and memorizing the stories, lives and pictures of the greatest modern artists. I still do, and have a hard time choosing between a great restaurant and a great museum; fortunately, now great museums host great restaurants!

What Makes People Happy?

A team of psychologists and economists reported in academic publication, *Science,* what many of us know but don't always admit: watching TV is a very enjoyable way to pass the time, but taking care of children is often as much fun as housework.

The study asked 909 women living in Texas to use a novel questionnaire that probes the moment-to-moment emotions that constitute an ordinary day: the Day Reconstruction Method, with a diary listing everything from reading the newspaper in the morning to arguing with coworkers over lunch, or falling asleep with the socks on. Each activity was relived the next day and rated using 12 scales: how the subjects felt at the time, whether criticized, hassled, worried or warm, friendly and happy. In general the group had a slow start but soon experienced mild pleasure that increased through the day, with bouts of anger, anxiety or frustration. Sex, socializing with friends, and relaxing were rated most enjoyable; while commuting, housework, or facing a boss, were the least pleasurable. These women rated TV-watching high on the list, ahead of shopping and talking on the phone.

One of the most consistent findings in the study was how little difference money made. Job security, too, had little influence (this would be heresy in France!). And, contrary to previous research, it was found that divorcees reported being slightly more cheerful during the day than did married women.

Resting the Case for Pleasure

"No sane man can afford to dispense with debilitating pleasures; no ascetic can be considered reliably sane. Hitler was the archetype of the abstentious man. When the other krauts saw him drink water in the Beer Hall they should have known he was not to be trusted!" Author, A. J. Leibling, offered these insightful words.

Pleasure is not an "extra", or bonus bringing a little more soul to certain of our acts; it is a fundamental part of animal life. It is just as difficult to define as spirit, but nonetheless man is very conscious of it; it intervenes in relation with "need" in the regulation of major home-ostatic functions[75].

Pleasure is a potent drive inducing forms of behavior adapted to physiological needs, especially in the case of temperature regulation and food-and-water intake. Subjects try to maximize their pleasure – just like rats! Sensory pleasure is an incentive to useful behavior, and maximization of pleasure the answer to physiological conflicts –a.k.a. stress.

But we should be vigilant: bigots are everywhere. My late friend Bernard Zacharias, trombonist of the Sidney Bechet & Claude Luter jazz band, created an imaginary principality in the heart of France; its motto was *Stultitia cinget* (approximately: '*we are surrounded by stupid people*').

Since I am [mostly] dealing with nutrition, remember that misinterpretation of reliable scientific findings is a major cause of abnormal nutrition behavior. Overreaction to health messages may precipitate such conditions as *anorexia nervosa,* or nutrient toxicity. Adverse food reactions, real or more often imagined, lead to restriction in food selection. Excessive austerity in food –and wine- use negates the pleasure of eating, a useful mechanism in food choice ensuring food diversity – and pleasurable health.

It is not by chance that most people toast as
Salute/Salud/Santé (GOOD HEALTH)

CHARITABLE GIVING FROM BOOK PROCEEDS

When living an authentic sensual life, your senses reveal exquisite beauty and offer rich pleasures.

At the same time, there exists a violent and horror-filled world where there are those who can only experience fear and pain.

A percent of all proceeds from this book, *Authentic Sensual Living,* and profits from Amorosa Bella, Dr. Charlyn Belluzzo's online luxury marketplace, are invested as charitable contributions in the following non-profit organizations that address the dreadfulness of sex slavery.

Alliance to Stop Slavery and End Trafficking – ASSET
www.assetcampaign.org/media

Children of the Night
www.childrenofthenight.org/home.html

Sex slavery and human trafficking is far more common than you might realize; it is an ugly thread woven into contemporary society that we "numb" ourselves from recognizing most of the time.

Thousands of women and children, girls and boys are "recruited" into this sickening practice through countless scams that use the appearance of wealth, travel, luxury gifts, designer clothes, expensive cars, and the elite nightclub scene.

Sometimes, even the promise of cigarettes is enough enticement to lure some young people into becoming victims in the crime of forced prostitution or subservience.

The most vulnerable are those most at risk.

If your charitable economic guidelines allow you to do so, please join Dr. Charlyn Belluzzo in donating additional monies to the organizations listed above.

ACKNOWLEDGEMENTS

First and foremost, I extend my forever love and gratitude to Rick, my journey partner, my adorable husband, toughest editor, and lifelong friend; thank you for allowing me to share our intimate stories, personal challenges, and hard fought victories with all of you, the readers.

I sincerely express my love and appreciation to my children, Riley and Karli Henneman. As a young single mother, I enjoyed growing up with you. You raised me, as I raised you. It has always been an adventure!

My special thanks goes to my friend and inspiration, Brenda Richard. Brenda embodies the essence of living an authentic sensual life. We spent many hours sharing our points of view and stories, living fully present in the moment, experiencing many facets of life, giving freely of temporal and emotional gifts, many of them captured in the pages of this book.

My earnest appreciation goes to a small circle of family and friends whose encouragement and confidence buoyed me up as I created this manuscript. These very special people recognized my need to tell my story and write a lifestyle book although my professional career has been academic, medical and research oriented, or philanthropic.

To Nisandeh and Vered Neta, I offer my appreciation for facilitating their book-writing course, *How to Write a Book in 28 Days*, which I attended in the Netherlands. Without their proven formula and concise instructions, I would not have felt I had the capacity to undertake the daunting task of writing a non-fiction book.

Thank you to those whose stories I have included in this book, along with my own. Your stories are exemplary and bring my principles to life.

Finally, I acknowledge you, my readers. Your time is a gift. You sat with me and share my writings. You contemplated my views and compared them to your own. Thanks to you!

Made in the USA
Charleston, SC
10 December 2009